GET TO

# THE PUBLISHING PUNCHLINE

A Fun (*and slightly aggressive*) 30-Day Guide
To Get Your Book Ready For The World

## JOY EGGERICHS REED

**PUNCHLINE**
PUBLISHERS

First Paperback Edition June 2021

Cover Design and Illustrations by Kristin McNess Moran

Illustrations Copyright © 2021 by Punchline Publishers

ISBN: 978-1-955051-03-3

ISBN (Mobi): 978-955051-01-9

ISBN (EPUB): 978-1-955051-02-6

Published by Punchline Publishers

punchlineagency.com

@JoyEggerichs

@PunchlineAgency

If you want to put a book out into the world but don't know where to start, this is the guide you need! Full of information and loaded with witty quips to keep you entertained while you get the scoop on all things writing and publishing from one of the best literary agents in the business.

Kristin and Danny Adams, authors of *The Road to Love and Laughter: Navigating the Twists and Turns of Life Together*

Joy gives readers a fun and fascinating tour through the maze of book publishing, helping current and hopeful writers understand what it takes to publish a book in a competitive landscape. She's a strategic thinker, a clear communicator, and an encouragement to so many writers, including myself. I hope others benefit from Joy's wisdom as much as I have.

Katelyn Beaty, editor, journalist, and author of *A Woman's Place: A Christian Vision for Your Calling in the Office, the Home, and the World*

Let me tell you this—you will NOT read a book about writing and publishing that will be as helpful and funny and awesome as Joy's. Not only is she seasoned and so helpful and wise, but man this book is just plain fun to read! Handing this to all aspiring authors from now on!

Jefferson Bethke, NYT best selling author of *Take Back Your Family: From the Tyrants of Burnout, Busyness, Individualism and the Nuclear Ideal*

Joy is the book proposal guru you've been waiting for. I can't even begin to explain how helpful this book would have been at the beginning of my writing and publishing journey! Let Joy be your guide!

Tiffany Bluhm, author of *Prey Tell: Why We Silence Women Who Tell the Truth and How Everyone Can Speak Up*

Joy gets straight to the publishing punchline with this clear, insightful and humorous guide for writers. The book industry can be a tricky one to navigate; Joy's practical guide demystifies the publishing process whilst communicating precisely what's required to catch the attention of an agent or publisher. If you're in need of a publishing cheerleader, a faithful advocate, or just to lighten up a little about it all - this book is for you!

Leah Boden, author of *Modern Miss Mason: Sharing Charlotte Mason with a New Generation (2022)*

Listen. Maybe there are books out there that will teach you how to write a book proposal, but I'm willing to bet none that will make it feel like you've got a straight-shooting, cheerleading bestie by your side every step of the way. This part of the book writing journey is hard. (I found it to be more challenging than actually writing the book!) But you CAN have some fun along the way. And if you don't hate fun AND getting ish done, read this book.

Liz Forkin Bohannon, CEO of Sseko Designs and author of *Beginner's Pluck: Build Your Life of Purpose and Impact Now*

If you have a book inside of you, the best thing is to sit down and start writing it. The second best thing is to read this book! Spend some time with Joy, a literary agent and your new best friend, and learn how to turn your insights into a sellable title.

Jonathan Collins, cofounder of BibleProject and coauthor of *Why Emotions Matter*

I was so entertained while reading it that I forgot I was learning about publishing. Read this book. You won't regret what you learn and all the laughs along the way.

*Tristen Collins, licensed professional counselor, Wayfinder coach and coauthor of Why Emotions Matter*

A must-have resource in making your book dreams into published realities. Joy is an invaluable guide and the literary coach you want in your corner. She's one of the main reasons I'm a published author today.

*Scott Erickson, author of Honest Advent and Say Yes*

Get To The Publishing Punchline is an approachable and important read for any aspiring author. It is a witty source of goal setting motivation and practical how-tos, mixed with a healthy dose of literary world reality. By following Joy's prompts, I believe every writer can gain confidence and discover their own unique voice for the world to read. It is a treasure trove of information to equip and inspire a first-time author like me.

*Marcy Gregg, Punchline author and speaker*

Packed with actionable steps for making the overwhelming process feel possible–and even fun. How cool to have an agent give us all a peek behind the curtain of how to craft a truly effective book proposal. Thank you, Joy!

*Scott Andrew James, indie book publishing guide and author of Amazon best seller Whatever Magic You Need*

Prepare to be entertained, encouraged, and challenged. Joy's enthusiasm is contagious–if you do the work in this book, you'll have a real proposal at the end of it, and have fun doing it!

*Elizabeth Knox, founder of MatchPace and Punchline author and speaker*

Writing a book is an overwhelming, brutal, and terrifying adventure. The process is so daunting most of us never get past the dreaming stage. That's why I am really excited about this book. Joy takes you through a journey/bootcamp/funny as hell process that will help you not just write a book but publish, market, and SELL your book. If you know you have a book in you but don't know where to start, my best advice would be to work through Joy's process! This book is a gift to authors, agents, and writers to be!

*Rick McKinley, lead pastor of Imago Dei Community and author of Faith For This Moment*

So much "how-to" or "DIY" advice comes without the accessibility, cleverness, and expertise that characterizes Joy Eggerichs's book. Her years of experience as a writer herself, as well as in relationship with countless authors, shows up in this book. It is helpful and kind and empowering. If you're wanting to put your words in the world, you should read this.

*Justin McRoberts, author of It Is What You Make of It*

It seems like the only people getting book deals these days are influencers, yet there are so many people with influence who have something important to share. Joy wrote this book for those people. It's a direct and tactical guide that feels like hard-earned secrets from your fun big sister.

Callie Murray, founder of Groundsweller

Joy provides an incredible game plan for aspiring authors to execute on their writing journey. This book leaves no room for other guides. Heed her advice and you will cross the finish line!

Daron K. Roberts, author of *Call an Audible* and *A Kids Book About Empathy*

I've always thought that the "Who" is more important than the "What." If writing a book is a personal goal, it's going to be the guide that gets you through the pain. While not everyone has access to such a brilliant literary agent like Joy, the world would be a better place if they did: that's why Joy's book is so important. Joy's voice rings true as she guides writers as if she was in the room. This book is going to yield fruit for YOU! Buy it and write!

Ben Sand, CEO of The Contingent and author of *A Kids Book About White Privilege*

Publishing is a journey marked by hard work and often high reward, but it's never easy, and it makes all the difference to have good guides. Consider this a guide you can trust. Joy breaks down every step of the process and empowers you on your way.

Stephanie Duncan Smith, senior editor for Baker Books

There is nothing more discouraging than having a big dream to write a book . . . and no idea where to start. Have no fear! Joy is here—and ready to provide positive, practical, and encouraging wisdom that will get you from dream to reality.

Nicole Unice, author of *The Miracle Moment: How Tough Conversations Can Actually Transform Your Most Important Relationships*

An extremely helpful book that provides tools to help writers understand their process, as well as exercises to get the writing process rolling. Joy's voice is distinct and conversational, while her humor brings a sense of comfort for something that can feel so overwhelming even before pen hits paper or fingers hit keys. This book is not only good for the literary world, but also very helpful to me as a songwriter.

Liz Vice, singer and songwriter

The book writing process was incredibly helpful to understand my voice, understand what resonated with audiences as a speaker, and identify the stories I wanted and needed to tell. Joy's book will help you not only as a writer, but as an overall communicator!

Terri Broussard Williams, author of *Find Your Fire: Stories and Strategies to Inspire the Changemaker Inside You*

To Holly, Amelia, and Kristin


Thank you for making this fun.
(Even though it was *slightly* aggressive.)

# TABLE OF CONTENTS

**CAN'T LIVE WITHOUT 'EM** *(NETWORK AND ENDORSEMENTS)*
**WHO'S YOUR OPRAH?** *(FOREWORD)*
**WHAT'S THE PLAN, STAN?** *(MARKETING PLAN AND BOOK LAUNCH)*

# BONJOUR!

## WHO IS THIS JOY CHARACTER, ANYWAY?

As a literary agent, I see book proposals that, unfortunately, I write off after about sixty seconds of skimming.

*Wow, Joy, that's harsh.*

I know, but there are specific things I look for that show me immediately how seriously a writer takes their goals of getting published. Content, clarity, and even aesthetics of a proposal speak volumes to me because it's a foreshadowing of how easy or difficult it will be for me to get on board and sell this book or idea to a publisher. And that *is* the role of an agent—to get so pumped about your book that they can't see straight and want to shout about it from the rooftops. So, if I can't see what you're getting at in your proposal, then it zaps my enthusiasm and I just can't move forward with it.

*Didn't know you took it so personally.*

I do! Because I want this process to be exciting—for both of us! The beginning to end process of getting a book into the world can feel daunting, so I want to demystify the work you need to do and make this first part FUN, so the rest feels easier.

*Fun?*

Yes, fun. Why not? Just because this is work doesn't mean it has to feel like filling out your taxes. Remember, you want to write because you are passionate about getting an idea, story, or topic into the world. Yet, I often hear writers say they don't know where to even start writing and crafting because writing a book feels overwhelming. One author I worked with to help her knock out a proposal in 30 days said that before we started, she thought she was getting a hernia. Another said they were keeping a trash-can next to their desk, you know—*just in case.*

*Sounds like you're a real peach to work with, Joy.*

It's only because I push people who I know can do it! And you wouldn't have picked up this book if you didn't have some level of belief in your-self too. I firmly believe that even if you don't decide to go the traditional publishing route, the practice of these prompts will help clarify your mes-sage, voice, platform, and more, resulting in confidence about what you are trying to say and to whom.

*So I could write for more people than just my mom?*

Well, that's up to you. If your mom controls the algorithm that decides who makes the *New York Times* Best Seller list, then she might not be the worst target audience. If she isn't, I promise you that this process will give you traction, help you get in a rhythm of writing, and push you to hit goals that will make the entire process flow that much smoother as you work towards getting your book published.

Tell your mom to get ready. She's got some reading to do.

## YOUR WORK, OUR FRIENDSHIP

If you are reading this book, then you probably also want to write and publish a book of your own one day. Maybe this book is still in a dreaming stage, with small sections already secretly written in your mind. Or, maybe you *have* written your book and show it to anyone you can at your annual holiday gatherings.

Wherever you're at in your book writing process, after you read this introduction, you'll find each section of this book is filled with prompts to help you make immense progress as an author in only 30 days.

If you complete this book and answer the prompts given to you each day, I can promise you at least three things:

1. You will have everything for an eye-catching proposal to present to agents and publishers.

2. You will find clarity on your own voice and reasons for writing.

3. You will know more about which publishing route is right for you.

I have already guided several authors-to-be through this material through small cohorts, and this has been some of the feedback:

> *"I feel like this plucked me off the dark and foggy path of trying to understand publishing, and catapulted me to a bright, wide-open place of confidence and excitement about the next steps." - Rachael Mitchell*

> *"The guidance you have given has been priceless. What has been learned and accomplished in 30 days is not lost on me–it is literally a life-long dream come true to have even come this far. It has given me so much reassurance for the path I am moving forward on. It has literally been game changing." - MacKenzie Koppa*

> *"It was more than I expected, and it reignited hope in me. Thank you." - Paige Allen*

> *"This has truly lit a fire in my spirit that had been slowly going out. Thank you for the opportunity to be reminded why I love writing." - Leslee Stewart*

> *"Joy designed a process that helped us save massive amounts of time by skipping wrong roads and catapulting over a lot of areas I've gotten mired down in before." - Jodi Cowles*

You might be thinking, "Ooo, a cohort. *That* would be great." And look, I know this is a book and not the same thing as working alongside other writers, but you could!

## How?

I promise if you put a post on social media that says, "Any friends out there ever thought of writing a book?" you will hear from several. My cohorts had a limit of five people, and I've found that to be the perfect amount—it didn't feel overwhelming when asking for advice, and there were just enough people to offer encouragement and feedback. If you're worried about not knowing anyone who lives close, you should know that we also never met in person and were located all over the world! (I currently live in Paris for my husband's job, so if the Eiffel Tower and baguette on the cover confused you, that's why. But, also, I really love bread, so if we ever move back to the U.S., I feel like the cover will still be 50 percent accurate. More on Paris, later.) Our cohort used my favorite app, Marco Polo, and met there for 30 days as the members went through all of the prompts you are about to work through.

If you've ever tried to write before, you've probably felt alone. This is a common experience for many of the writers I work with, so that's why I encourage you to find friends. However, if you don't want to cast the net on the socials just yet, maybe . . . I could be your friend?

*We don't even know each other, Joy.*

True. However, my hope with this book is the people who read and complete it alone might just hear my voice in the same way my authors (hopefully) hear my voice as their literary agent: friendly, and slightly aggressive. I write like I talk, so if you can imagine the voice of an alto/tinge-of-a-midwest-accent/self-diagnosed-asthmatic type, then I think you'll be able to hear me quite perfectly in your head.

And until I get to know you better, I thought maybe I should tell you a bit about myself. After that, you can dive into the work and writing part of this whole book. Or, I guess you can skip ahead and just do that now. I won't take it personally.

## MY LIFE'S STORY (MORE OR LESS)

"I'm a literary agent that doesn't read," I say to the authors I represent. It's half joking, but also mostly true. I say this because so many of the agents and editors I know in this business came into it due to their love of literature. They post photos on social media of the forty-seven books they've read this month, and while I have read *twenty-three* this month, most of them rhyme and are recommended to me by my two-year-old.

Why I *am* good at what I do is because: I (generally) enjoy humans, I know a good book idea when I hear it, I love being a hype-girl for voices that need to be heard, I am never afraid to ask the question everyone is thinking, and I will push tactfully and truthfully for what I want. My Strengths Finder results *did* compare me to Hillary Clinton, so I'll leave it at that for now.

Shall we start from the beginning so I can explain to you how I sort of fell into this industry?

*Sure.*

My father is a *New York Times* Best Selling author and has sold millions of books. When he got his first book deal back in the early 2000s and I was in college, he let me sit in on some of the meetings with agents and publishers. I heard the questions they would ask, the angles they would want him to write his book from, and had a front row seat to watching a first-time author trying to get this one possible shot exactly right.

After I graduated college, I began working for my father, and as a result, attended publisher meetings where he gave me the opportunity to speak up, ask questions, and soak it all in. My father is a brilliant communicator, and seeing how he shares a vision and a message brewing within him is moving—not to mention how he honors all the people in the room, and toggles between deferring to publishers expertise while staying true to the content he wants to put out into the world. As a Communications Studies major, it was not only a crash course in publishing, but a real world masterclass on effective communication.

I wasn't my father's literary agent at that point, though. Let's be honest—he believes in me, but even I wouldn't have let twenty-two-year-old Joy take the reins on negotiating royalties and subsidiary rights. At that stage in the game, I had just started directing all of my parents' live events for their organization (my mom speaks too), and I loved it. If you can't tell from the direction of this book and what we are about to engage in together, let me clarify something about my personality—I like to tell people what to do and make them do it in an orderly fashion.

Before I started working for my parents, they would show up at an event to speak, and were essentially at the mercy of the host's ability or inability to run an event effectively. After I came on board, I created a forty-five-page document for hosts that included everything my parents needed for a successful event to happen: from volunteer coordination to marketing, registration to coffee breaks, and book signings to ticket sales. From six months out to two weeks after the event, and a minute-by-minute schedule for the actual day's events—this document had *it all*. When a host would contact me and ask me a question, I would kindly answer, but also in a slightly shaming way, refer them back to Pg. 26 for the answer.

My kids are in for a really chill childhood.

"Oh, you don't know how to clean the toilets, Millie? Please reference Pg. 42 of the Reed Family Chores Manual. I've CC'd your father on this so you can ask him any outstanding questions about trash removal."

I didn't tell you what my parents speak about, did I? No, I didn't.

They speak about marriage, and at the time I was directing their speaking events, I was very, VERY much single. (Outside of the one time I almost got married to a guy, realized he was actually not a good dude, left for Switzerland to get away from him, broke my ankle on a very non-dangerous part of an Alp because I'm *super smart* and thought I would "snowboard on a sled," and spent a couple months in a Chalet on the side of an Alp trying to physically and emotionally heal. But that story is for another book.)

So, back to my singleness. When I directed these events, so many people would come through the book signing line and say, "I wish I would have known about this stuff twenty years ago! If only I knew then what I know now."

Over time (and by over time, I mean after running off to the Alps and being an idiot), I decided that maybe, in the midst of my brokenness (in more ways than one) I could try to help my generation learn what my parents were teaching now, and not have regret for twenty years wasted.

My parents, who believe in me more than they should, said, "YES!"

I had all sorts of theories and ideas about what was wrong with our generation, what my failed relationship had taught me, how we could communicate better, why we all had unrealistic expectations, and on and on.

Unfortunately, the only people listening to me were my parents. Primarily my father, who would graciously listen to my hypotheses and action plans. He encouraged me to start reading research, studying, and interviewing my peers about singleness and relationships. (Probably so he could get off the phone.) He also told me to start putting my thoughts to paper, so my thoughts, which seemed so WILDLY clear to me as I rambled away, could really be fine-tuned.

He essentially told me that the practice of writing and developing a talk for an audience would help me clarify my message. He described a point of resolve he would feel when the point he was trying to make became clear. I was a Communication Studies major, and loved good rhetoric and people with incredible stage presence. This was something I was energized at just the idea of doing. And with a blow to my ego, my dad said:

"But no one is asking you to come speak. So, start writing." Ouch.

## THE JOYS OF WRITING, OR, MORE OUCH

A bit about my writing background . . . (besides my obvious undying love and overuse of ellipses and parentheticals).

In high school, my memories of writing were centered in Freshman English when I had to read some paper in front of the class with my friend Carmella while wearing my newly acquired scoliosis brace. Outside of occasionally pinching my backside when sitting down in my chair and letting out a little yelp, most people didn't know I had a brace. That is, until sweet Carmella, always up for a good time, thought it would be funny to kick things off by knocking on my stomach and saying, "Look everybody, Joy has abs of steel!"

More like abs of overpriced plastic that had been shaped and padded to align my spine, minimize oxygen intake, and increase my chances of never getting asked to prom. So, the main takeaway I have from Freshman English is the mind's ability to retain nothing when you black out due to embarrassment.

Another English class I took my junior year was with a teacher who was in her final year and about to retire. My takeaway from that class was how much I enjoyed watching movies and how few questions on-the-brink-of-retirement teachers have about your twenty-minute leave of absence to "go to the bathroom."

I also have a faint memory of taking a journalism class, and my main take-away from that was that I knew very early on I would not be a journalist. Formatting those little columns was way too difficult.

Fast forward to college, and I started to take my writing more seriously. Even with my intentions of tackling important topics in higher education, my writing was still terrible. I vividly remember reading, "This isn't high-school anymore," written in bold red pen on the back of one of my papers. Ouch again.

I wanted to respond, "Apparently it is, because I was a terrible writer then too!"

———————

So when my dad told me I had to write in order to speak, I wanted to yell, "But I'm a COMMUNICATIONS MAJOR! I want to TALK!"

Again, zero times zero people were clamoring to hear me speak, so I got myself a blog and started writing. As you know, writing can either flow out of you like sweet honey, or it can feel like you're bringing your leg up around your neck and voluntarily slamming your entire self onto a wres-tling mat as self-inflicted torture. Whether we write because it's a medium to fine-tune a message, or we do it because we love the craft, it simply takes time. Discipline, and time. That's what makes it so hard to do.

I hear so many people talk about the book they want to write, or are going to write, and the cynic in me thinks, "Mmmhmm. Tell me when you've actually put pen to paper or opened your computer and started."

But, you, my soon to be friend (and my hope is that we will be friends by the end of this), are

DOING IT. You've opened this book, you're reading my words, and partaking in my story. Most importantly, you're finally listening to that compelling feeling you've had to get your message out and into the world.

My blogging, and then vlogging (or whatever the kids might be calling it this day), did eventually lead to speaking requests. Even though I had lacked so much confidence in the writing department, the practice of consistently blogging multiple times a week (for no one but my parents at first), having my writing edited and critiqued, and returning to write and rewrite did help clarify my voice. Then, whether it was on the page or the stage, I found that sense of resolve that my father spoke about, faster and faster.

"Writers love to have written" is a phrase many of us have heard—and it's true. But, I'm hoping we can enjoy this process together, because I can tell you that while I was someone who hated writing and rarely read, I have also grown to live in and enjoy a world immersed with both the writing and the "have written."

After several years of blogging and speaking, I was approached by a publisher to write a book. I was deeply honored and wildly terrified that my ghosts of English professors past would reach out to said publisher to let them know the truth. Insecurity made me laugh the inquiry off.

"I'm too young to write a book of any significance. They just want me to write a book because my dad was successful at writing. It's low risk for them as my last name will sell enough to make back their advance."

*No offense, but that's exactly what I was thinking too, Joy.*

Well, I'm glad we are already at that point in our relationship where you can be brutally honest with me.

But, maybe my writing *had* improved, or maybe the publishers liked my message and knew with enough editorial work and actually turning the spell check function on my computer to ON, we'd have a decent shot.

Whatever the reason, I remember telling all of the above hesitations to my father, who I was sure would say, "Yes, you need to wait. I didn't write a book until after the age of 50 and some grey hairs. That's when wisdom comes, and that will also give you another 25 years of writing practice."

But he didn't. He said, "Go for it. You have a book to write for your generation about your experiences and with your voice."

"Really!?" I said with a nervous pit in my stomach, like Carmella had just struck again.

"Yes. And I think you have enough connections in this industry to agent the book yourself. You should give it a try."

I'd like to take a moment to slow clap for all the parents, and especially fathers of young women, who voice their unwavering belief in their abilities. It can change the trajectory of your kid's life if you just take the time to say it out loud. And for those of you who didn't have a parent cheering you on, let me say to you, in the words of one of the Lost Boys in Robin Williams's acclaimed film, *HOOK*: [1]

"You're doing it, Peter!!!"

You are, and you can.

(Ok, more of supporting you later. This is still the part of the book where I'm being a little self-indulgent.)

So, I started putting together a type of pitch about what I would write for my book. Since I had preexisting relationships at the different publishers from working with my dad, I made personalized videos for each of them and told them my idea instead of writing the traditional book proposal.

[1]  Acclaimed by the Screen Actors Guild of only Joy Eggerichs Reed

Yes, having those relationships helped me jump through hoops as a first-time author *much* more easily than other people. However, the reason I now love the process of a book proposal is because it helps writers hyper-focus on what they are trying to say—to whom and how. I didn't have to do everything I will encourage you to do when I went through the publishing process, BUT I am convinced if I had done it all, the actual writing process of the book would have been much easier.

After sending the videos, I was now in full-fledged negotiation mode. I received offers from all of the publishers I pitched to, and compared the pros and cons that I saw between them. I had meetings with publishing teams and tried to figure out who would be the most beneficial to work with in light of the areas that I lacked.

Humorously, I even told one publisher that I had a dream of waking up in a room surrounded by stacks of my own book one day, and they surprised me with a VERY significant amount of author copies in their offer.

I finally pulled the trigger with the team I thought was the most engaged and excited to work with me. Once the contract was signed, I received half my advance. I had never had a check in my hands for that much money, and boy did it feel good!

And then, the weight of writing my book sank in . . .

All of my ideas were in my head, no outline or chapter summaries had been written. I was staring at a blank screen and a blinking cursor. It was time to back it up.

This was when I essentially started the process of a proposal similar to the one you will complete throughout this book. I ended up doing most of the work I'm encouraging you to do, just out of order.

## THE IMPORTANCE OF A WRITING COMMUNITY (WHO MAY ALSO DOUBLE AS MATCHMAKERS)

I called in the troops, and had my colleague and friend Stephanie help me outline and order the structure of the book. We all have to figure out what works best for our own writing practice, but for me, it was so beneficial to have skilled friends along the way. Stephanie is a great question asker and is highly skilled organizationally. She knew my goals with the book, so she gave me prompts, got me talking, and then, on the wall in our office which was entirely covered in whiteboard, we outlined my book.

The process provided clarity, and I was so grateful to Stephanie that I took some of my advance money and bought her a bike. I only share this because it conjures up a funny story that I have nowhere else to tell but here . . . but feel free to skip ahead if you aren't interested in hearing stories that otherwise have nothing to do with this book and writing process.

I had bought the bike off Craigslist, but I took her to a local bike shop to pick out those fancy clip-in shoes and other bike accessories to get her ready for the road.

The guy at the bike shop that was helping us was pretty cute, so Stephanie, not one to only assist with book writing, was trying to make a love connection. His actual name was James Brown. This made both of us laugh because, well, his parents definitely would have known when naming him that they were setting him up for a life of people, upon learning his name, either saying, "Like the singer?" or just full on busting into, "Owwwww-weeeeeee! I feel good, dun-nu-nu-nu-nuhhhh."

He said he was new to the area, so Stephanie used that as an "in" to make the match. It was a very long time ago and I don't completely remember how it happened, but one of us had the other's number by the time we finished paying for Stephanie's fancy shoes.

I was in a season of staying open to anything, so I tried to say yes to any matchmaking from friends, and even random dates with men named after famous singers. James Brown and I made plans to meet at a place that I knew would have lots of people and pool tables, so if talking got awkward, I could just reveal my highly competitive side to hopefully make him uncomfortable enough to end the night early.

As we talked, I realized that this would never be anything more than just a friendship. I started to think it would perhaps be even less than a friendship as he started telling me his love for true crime YouTube videos. RED FLAAAAAAAAAAAAG.

To be fair, I think we got on this topic because I was in the middle of a month-long stint of serving on a Grand Jury One—which was just gnarly. There was a small group of us who heard from victims, sometimes criminals, and police officers immediately after the most serious crimes in our city have happened. (Think *murder*.) We were free to Matlock style interrogate people who sat only feet away from us in a small room. Our copious note-taking was vital to the District Attorney's office since many cases don't go to trial for a long time. Once the case went to trial, if testimonies and stories changed, let's just say…

DUN. DUN. DUHHHHHHHHHHHHH.

As you can see, I was very enmeshed in this process and probably brought the dark conversation upon myself, but all that to say, I didn't stay on the date long and happily used my backup excuse of something I needed to get to when the true crime conversation continued for just a little beyond my level of comfort.

Fast forward to the next morning at 7 a.m.: I looked at my phone only to see several very early morning missed calls from Mr. James Brown. I listened to his voicemails to find out that he and his other friend had, in his words, been attacked in a bar fight late last night and he needed my help with what they should do.

I reflected on how I must have really sounded like an expert the night prior, spouting legal jargon with a level of confidence that caused this near stranger to want my counsel.

A normal woman in her late twenties probably wouldn't call back, and just conclude this was an unwise situation to engage in. But again, there are times in my life where I mix unfounded confidence with a desire to help, and the next thing I knew, I was meeting with plaintiff J. Brown and his friend outside a local coffee shop, eating donuts, analyzing their black eyes and flesh wounds, and giving them pro-bono legal aid.

After that, I cut ties with Mr. Brown, but you better believe I can't hear "Get up offa that thing" without fond memories of Bike Boy and Stephanie's large chasm of skill between literary assistance and match-making.

Remember kids, just say "YES" to writing in community, and "NO" to the forty-seven calls before 7 a.m.

## BACK TO THE BOOK BASICS

The next steps for writing my book were to carve out time for concentrated solo writing. Many writers will say they observe a daily practice of writing. An hour a day in the morning or night, depending on their creative rhythms, or even because it's the only time they can find between carpool, work, and meals.

For me, I can't do that. I need big chunks of time with absolute silence or wordless classical tunes, no email or phone, and ideally, for several days in a row. I plotted out, based on my manuscript deadlines, four writing retreats over the course of nine to twelve months. After I got a majority of the book written, I called in my friend Lyndsay to join me for one of the retreats to help me heighten the humor aspect of my writing.

My ideas and writing are funny in my own head, but I always feel more confident when someone who I think is funnier and a better writer (Lyndsay) can either pat me on the back in approval, or say, "What if you said it this way . . ." That's when I feel the energy in the room crank up, as well as the number of jokes.

See, the writing process can be hard work, but it doesn't have to be un-fun work. Bring in the music, coffee, or friends that you need to create an environment that reminds you that you WANT to write, that the process is worth it, and the birth that you will give to this book will be a creative feat and something you can be proud of.

Your book becomes like those little 26.2 mile stickers that marathon runners put on the back of their car, except instead of running for five hours, you just need to flip to page 262. You can say, "I did that . . . I wrote that many pages, and I only fell to the ground with leg cramps twice."

## FINDING A LOVE FOR PUBLISHING THROUGH [ALMOST] PUBLISHING MY BOOK

As I trudged through the writing process, I worked closely with the publisher on cover design, endorsements, and marketing ideas. I can be very particular about design, and had a friend whom I knew I wanted to do the cover. I wanted it to be black and white with gold leaf accents. At that time (around 2013), there weren't a ton of authors in my genre of books coming out with black covers. I was determined to make this happen, and eventually the publisher graciously let me have my way. And I still love the design, this many years later. Things were finally coming together for my very first book.

*So where can I get a copy of this book, Joy?*

Oh, you're so kind. I knew I liked you.

Well, I finished the manuscript . . . but chose to not turn it in and sent the advance back six months before it was to be released.

*WHAT?!*

Yeah. I know. Sometimes I still wonder if it was the right move, but here's what I can tell you: there was some heavy turnover happening at the publisher I was working with, and I kept waiting for the editor they were supposed to find me to dive in on my project and give it the attention it needed. (Remember, I can't spelle.)

As I waited longer and longer, I started to get insecure that the publisher was banking on my last name to sell the book, and that they didn't actually care about the quality of the product we were putting out as much as I had hoped. Looking back, I believe they did care about my book; it was just a combination of bad timing and not getting the answers or affirmation I was looking for from an editor to truly be confident in my book.

Simultaneously, I started feeling like the process of writing was meant for more than just producing a book to put into the world. It was a practice that actually brought about personal healing, reflection, and growth. Not to mention, being my own agent opened my eyes to the fact that I liked that process of getting a book into publishers' hands: advocating for a message, brainstorming creative elements of the project, strategic marketing, and the odd love and fascination with contracts. The legal department was like, "This girl has watched one too many episodes of Matlock." And I was like, "OR SERVED ON A GRAND JURY AND KNOWS THE LAW OF THE LAND!"

You know that sense of resolve I talked about? I never felt it as I wrote that last chapter. I kept trying and trying, but I knew it wasn't right. That feeling, mixed with no editor and an impending deadline, had me headed to the bank asking for a cashier's check in the amount of the advance money I had been paid.

When the teller came back to the window with the check, she said with enthusiasm in her voice, "Ohhh, you must be buying something fun!" And, in the most Matlock sounding voice I could muster . . .

*[cue camera zooming in on my face as I slowly turn and break the fourth wall, looking at the audience to say]*

"Yes. My freedom."

DUN. DUN. DUHHHHHHHHHHHHHH. (Again.)

But, here we are, almost a decade later, and I am now a literary agent with a book manuscript on my computer (that I should probably back up) and a deep empathy for the hills and valleys of the book writing process. I've been in your shoes, and can empathize with you every step of the way.

Now, I've written this to help you get to your end result in a more-fun and less back-tracky way than I did.

*Thanks, Joy.*

You're welcome, friend.

## TO FEAR OR NOT TO FEAR

*But, Joy, this is scary! I'm getting a hernia just thinking about putting a book into the world.*

I know. Sometimes when I think back to my book and breaking my contract, I wonder if it was really because I felt like the ending wasn't right and the book was being forced, or if I really had fear about putting my words into the world . . . FOREVER.

It was probably a mix of both.

But, there is a morbid motivator I come back to when I'm filtering what projects to take on:

"We're all going to die."

*Wow. Didn't see that coming in a book marketed as "Write a book proposal, and have FUN doing it!"*

I know it's a little startling, but it's true, and I find this mantra freeing at times. One time my husband and I were weighing the pros and cons of something he was considering, and I said, "Is there a world in which you can imagine yourself on your deathbed and having regret over _____?"

His answer was no, and we kept that filter in mind as we continued to weigh the pros and cons. We didn't immediately say YES, and that thing hasn't happened yet, but it helped us with perspective as we worked through the decision.

Maybe your book will get published by the imprint you've always dreamed of, maybe you'll print off twenty-five copies for friends and family at a local printer, or maybe you'll write the book and keep it on your computer, knowing the process and practice helped you to heal.

Whatever it ends up being, there is something inside of you that has a desire to get this story, this message, on the page. When you feel those nerves sneaking up on you and you grab the trash bin next to your desk at the thought of finally writing this book, ask yourself:

*"Is there a world in which I would be on my deathbed and regret having written this book?"*

If your answer is no, then let's get cracking. We've got some fun to do.

# LOGISTICS AND ENVIRONMENT

*FIND THE RIGHT TIME (AND PLACE, AND PEOPLE) FOR WRITIN' TIME!*

Before we get into the nitty gritty of writing your book, it's best to figure out what type of writer you are and the environment you need to be in. On top of that, you need your people! People who will support your endeavors because I am going to be asking a lot from you over the next 30 days. I KNOW you can do it because I've done it with tons of other writers and they have felt such a sense of accomplishment when they stuck to the schedule. Each section will give you the number of days I suggest you take to hit your goals. If you are the type of person who will wait until the last day to try and get all of your prompts finished, then even more so you need people to hold you accountable. Block off chunks of time on your calendar so you have the next 30 days allocated to this project.

*[Heads Up] Day 7-15 is a lot of writing. This is where we cover the three sample chapters that you will choose for including in your book proposal. Many of you are starting this project having already written a manuscript draft, and now you want to figure out how to organize and pitch it. Others have an idea living in your head and are wondering if there's enough there for a book. This process will help clarify what's in your head and you may discover it's more fitting as an article, online course, movie script, or holographic experience.*

*If you haven't written anything, I would encourage you to start today.*

*During the next couple days, you will pick a time and place for writing, so as you try out different options, get real words on the page. That will make your Day 7-15 much easier because you can go back and sift through what you've written and will have a sense of momentum. Even if you don't end up using what you've written or change directions, that's all part of the process.*

*In short: the next 30 days should be filled with doing the prompts AND getting as many words done on your manuscript as possible. The term "overachiever" gets a bad name, but not for this project and not in my book. (And this is my book.)*

*You can do it!*

*When you see this image of a hand throughout the book, it's simply highlighting for you an example (often made up by me) that would be seen in a traditional book proposal. The goal is to make writing the prompt that will typically follow the example that much easier for you. You don't have to follow it verbatim, but it's there to essentially prompt your prompt!*

*When you see this little Eiffel at the end of each prompt, you'll be able to see the progress you've made. As the tower fills in, you're that much closer to the top. . . and by top, I mean you'll have an incredible view of what your book will be!*

# WE AREN'T ALL HEMINGWAY
## A SCHEDULE THAT WORKS FOR YOU

As I mentioned before, I currently live in Paris. Yes, France. I have gotten by the last four years on a steady diet of warm baguettes with butter churned by the hands of a wrinkled old Frenchman named Jean Marc and I have no regrets.

When my husband and I were dating and I found out that he worked for a company whose parent company was headquartered in Paris, I said with all the shallowness I could muster, "Get a job transfer to Paris, and I'll marry you."

Thankfully, I married him before Paris was a reality for both of us, and now we can live in a happy marriage where my motives are not called into question. (Although I did demand that he grow a beard because I love beards, and now he hasn't shaved in five years. The shallowness lives on!)

After tying the knot and buying and furnishing our first home in America, Matt noticed a position open in the Paris office that was a perfect fit and career move for him. Next thing we knew, we were selling all our new furnishings, handing the keys of our dream home off to renters, and setting up as newlyweds in Paris.

Four years and two babies later, we talk about that first year in Paris and how much we crammed into our short "pre-diaper" time. We were like tourists on speed that year. When you get married later in life like we did, and then calculate all the time your friends who got married in their twenties had together before having kids, we knew whatever way we did the math, we would never catch up to the same amount of "just the two of us" time many of our friends had before welcoming *petite bébés* into the world. And when those same friends were shipping their kids off to college, we'd just be starting parent teacher conferences while flashing our AARP cards. We settled on one year: just the two of us tackling Paris together, with warm baguettes and butter in hand.

When we think back to that first year in Paris, we both agree that one of our favorite memories was taking Hemingway's *A Moveable Feast* with us to restaurants, park benches, and wherever we had a moment to read to each other about his life in Paris. It was as romantic as you'd imagine. Mostly because when comparing yourself to Hemingway's marriages, it can be wildly encouraging for two newlyweds that we were probably going to do better by the sheer fact that neither one of us had a big problem with going to the horse tracks and gambling away our income.

On one of our weekend adventures, we went to Brasserie Lipp, a cafe where Hemingway would drink beer and write. The aesthetics of the restaurant, more than any of his other writing haunts, have remained largely untouched. We drank an overpriced beer and imagined him sitting in the booth with his pencil and pad, writing stories of war and of rivers in Michigan.

We can often romanticize and idolize what writing should look like, especially if we compare ourselves to one of the greats; but from what I gather, while he was writing what would become canonical novels and short stories, Hemingway was often pretty buzzed, lived from paycheck to paycheck, and was frequently unfaithful to his wife.

You might not have the Brasserie Lipp in Sainte Germaine to fuel your creativity, and cheap wine might make you sleepy, but I would encourage you to find or create a space that you find most conducive to writing. Get that space as "ready" as possible so that when you're there, you feel like you can breathe, think, and write without distraction. If it's in your home and you have kids, I also strongly suggest making a sign for the door that has thinly veiled threats about entering when you're writing . . . OR ELSE.

Some of you might find that you need your writing space to change. You may thrive as you type among the hum of a busy coffee shop, a hipster loving coworking space, or the floor in the Historical Fiction aisle of your local library.

If you aren't sure how you write best, take one week to write in a consistent spot you've set up in your home, and take another week and try several different locations. You'll eventually figure out which environment is best suited to helping you focus.

Learning *where* you work best is important, but another crucial piece is knowing *when* you best work.

While Hemingway is most immortalized as writing and drinking from what are now landmark stops in Paris for literary lovers, from the sounds of it, Hemingway was still quite disciplined in writing when he was sharp in the morning:

*When I am working on a book or a story I write every morning as soon after first light as possible. There is no one to disturb you and it is cool or cold and you come to your work and warm as you write. You read what you have written and, as you always stop when you know what is going to happen next, you go on from there. You write until you come to a place where you still have your juice and know what will happen next . . . You have started at six in the morning, say, and may go on until noon or be through before that.*

Looks like Hemingway and I have more than just living in Paris in common. Mornings have always been the best writing time for me. If I was to write at night you'd find me coming-to three hours later with H, J, K, L keys indented on my right cheek.

BUT, this might not be you.

One of my authors, Elizabeth Knox, founder of MatchPace, a consulting firm that helps companies maximize effectiveness, explains in her forthcoming book why understanding individual employees' Chronotypes and allowing them to work accordingly will benefit the whole company.

*Chronotypes are the emotional and behavioral patterns associated with a person's internal clock. But these aren't set in stone—research indicates that your chronotype can change over the various seasons of your life. While you may have been able to focus late into the evening at one time of your life (like those all-nighters you pulled in college), new responsibilities and life circumstances may now require an adjusted sleep-wake pattern, shifting your peak focus period.*

*It is important to structure your day to ensure you are able to give your personal and professional best to the things most important to you. Structuring your work day for maximum effectiveness requires 1) planning how you'll spend your time and attention, and 2) using your peak performance times to your advantage.*

Sometimes we try to fit our writing habits into what Hemingway, or our fa-vorite author (who wrote this really great book on how to write a book pro-posal, cough-cough) does, instead of seeing their habits as just one method to try. Don't force something that isn't you OR your chronotype!

I will often hear people say that you just have to write something every day. One hour, two hours a day—"just sit down to write!" they say. Again, that's well intentioned and works for some people, but not for all. When I was working on my book, I had to, as I mentioned, do writing retreats with big chunks of writing, not little bits every day.

Even now, with this book, I'm writing on a day when I've turned my email off, flipped my phone over (for the most part) and blocked off 8 a.m.-1:30 p.m. to just write. I write for thirty to sixty minutes at a time, take a ten minute break, and get back to it.

Just like with your writing space, you have to try a few different methods; pay attention to your productivity and what makes writing most enjoyable for you. Hey, if it's cheap wine and writing after a night of betting on horse races, then I guess that works for you. But here's the thing that Hemingway did that many of us need reminding of: he wrote and wrote and made a practice of continuing to write, even when he thought what he was writing wasn't good.

Don't let your fears or hesitations about your writing keep you from find-ing the time and place that's best for you. Then, keep returning to it over and over until the book is finished.

In the space below, write out the times and spaces you want to try for writing. Where do you imagine getting the most work done? Will you have one "writing space," or move around? Do you work best in silence, or with quiet noise around you, like at a coffee shop? How much margin do you have in your life right now? If that answer is "none," is there something you can cut out for a while and put writing in its place?

Write "pros" and "cons" after you try each approach and space for writing. Fill in what you liked and what you didn't so you can figure out your "thing."

# WRITERS ANONYMOUS
## FINDING ACCOUNTABILITY AND SUPPORT

If you have not already told your family, roommates, parents, or dogs that you will be carving out some serious work time these next four weeks, now is the time. You might not have writing partners, but this process should not be done alone. It may simply be telling your family so they can help support you when you've figured out your writing rhythm and where you'll set up shop. It may also be asking a friend to check in with you, cheer you on, or hold you accountable if that's the kind of relationship you have. If you aren't good with timelines and goals, think of that annoying friend who has her day planned out minute by minute and ask her if she might help you find some (reasonable) deadlines for your process while, of course, factoring in all the variables of your life and time constraints we've talked about previously.

One of the reasons writers so often feel alone in this process is because they don't think through what they need as support and ask for it or invest in it. I'm not saying you need to take out a loan, book a three-month stint at the Ritz, and abandon your family, but maybe a stay at a small Airbnb on a farm thirty minutes outside of town, or just splurging for that fancy coffee drink to get you hyped up is the thing you need to invest in your writing.

Write down three names of people you want to tell about your book and how you might ask them to support you, or hold you accountable to your goals.

# WHAT'S YOUR DCS?
## WRITE IT AND BELIEVE IT

Do you ever get your colloquialisms mixed up? Just me?

One day, my husband overheard me saying to a client, "What's your Dream Case Scenario?" Later he said, "You know, you're combining two phrases together: *Dream Scenario* and *Best Case Scenario*. It's not *Dream Case Scenario*." And in that moment of loving critique, I realized that my word jumble had created something so special and next-level that humanity[2] inherently understood (or was too afraid to correct me on), and I needed to trademark DCS. IMMEDIATELY!

I've been asking people I work with what their Dream Case Scenario is ever since, and bless them, they always acted like they knew what I was talking about.

It's true though, don't you agree? When you ~~hear me say~~ read "Dream Case Scenario" you know it's *beyond* the best of scenarios, it's the scenarios all your wildest dreams are made of! Even my husband now asks me what my DCS(™) is, so I know it's catching on. At least in this household.

Start thinking about your book and your hopes as a writer. Don't be afraid to dream too big, and don't be afraid to throw humility aside for a moment. What feels like success for you as a writer and communicator?

---

[2] Five people

I've been noticing a trend from leaders I admire and successful companies: they write their goals down. Some on the back of scrap pieces of paper, and some on a document that they put out for the public. Either way, the recording of goals is a common practice among those who are successful and actually reach their goals.

Don't be afraid to put your DCS into the world. Or at a minimum, on the page below this sentence.

---

**PROMPT**

*Write out your DCS(™) in the space below.*

---

# YOUR AUDIENCE, YOUR VOICE

*QUICK, YOU HAVE UNTIL FLOOR 22!*

There's conflicting stories on where the term "elevator pitch" came from. Some believe it was coined in the old Hollywood days when a young aspiring writer would catch an unsuspecting executive on an elevator ride and corner them about their script idea that would be "Huge, I tell ya! Huge!"

A more recent story is about a writer at *Vanity Fair* in the 1990s who was always trying to pitch stories to the on-the-go editor in chief. To get her attention, the writer would wait for her to get on the elevator, join her and use that short ride to pitch her ideas. That's dedication and a whole lot more hanging around the elevator doors than I'd care to do, but I respect the strategy.

We are doing a lot less elevator riding these days, and social media has made it easier for us to get our ideas on the radar of people we don't share an office with, but the principle behind the elevator pitch remains the same.

1. Don't assume everyone is as excited about your idea as you are. Can you get them excited in thirty to ninety seconds while being metaphorically boxed out by the janitor and their industrial-size trash cans?

2. In those thirty to ninety seconds, would your idea, proposal, and story be clear enough for someone who doesn't know you from Adam, Eve, or Nancy Drew to understand, *and* then coherently relay your idea to someone else?

Here are three C's that probably aren't groundbreaking enough to give on an elevator pitch, but it should help you easily remember and filter out what to say or not say as you propose your idea.

The Three Magical C's are . . .

1. **CLEAR**

2. **CONCISE**

3. **COOL**

**CLEAR:** Even the most intricate of story lines or scientific theories can benefit from being summarized into a clear statement for the average human. Even if we are Einstein, when we *try* to make ourselves sound smart, assume everyone wants the obscure details, or can't get to our thesis or main points quickly and clearly, we may lose our audience, agents, or publishers from grasping what our end goal is. Think about that well written movie synopsis on *IMDb* vs. that detailed personal review on *Rotten Tomatoes*. We don't need ALL the details, Amanda. Even if a book or idea is very nuanced, the most brilliant writers and communicators know how to create a word picture or analogy that lets others in on the concept. Oh hey, *Concept*. Another C! How **C**razy! Woah. I **C**an't . . . stop . . . **C**oming . . . up . . . with . . .

*Joy, please stop.*

Moving on.

**CONCISE:** Don't add ~~extra~~ unnecessary ~~words and~~ details ~~no matter how many C's you Come up with or how excited you are about this book no one Currently Cares about but you.~~

**COOL:** Are you excited about your book!? It's good to show your enthusiasm and belief in the project. In short, don't play "too cool" when your idea is actually really . . . cool! Tell the world why you're pumped and passionate about this project, and watch others catch the vision.

*Cool. But, how can I do all this in thirty seconds, Joy??*

Other topics we cover in this section will center on clarifying your audience, voice, and additional details surrounding your project. As that clarity comes, so will the ability to tell it quickly. But we have to get through all the extra noise and doubt first.

One of the obstacles I hear from writers is the uncertainty they feel around their voice and idea. Writers are often creative by nature, and there are several book ideas or projects going at one time. Additionally, there are so many voices already out in the ether that we look to and wonder if our idea really IS as cool or clear as we thought it was when we first were struck with it. Insecurity creeps in as we wonder if we are just a poor man's copy of someone we like.

*Am I?*

I don't know, but I think wasting too much time on comparing ourselves to others (aka "imposter syndrome") isn't really going to benefit us much in this life. Unless you find comparison motivates and encourages you to be and do better, comparison usually leads to too much time spent on questioning our own originality, and is just a self-inflicted psychological detour.

Spend the brain space writing instead.

"Nothing is new under the sun," the book of Ecclesiastes says, so the reality is, someone has had a similar thought, life experience, or insight that you have had—but that shouldn't stop you. There is always a time to say it with fresh eyes, a fresh voice, and, frankly, an alive voice. And if you are alive, and something is in you to write, get it out. It might be for you, or it might be for the masses, but I doubt you'll regret getting it onto the page and if you do that, you'll start to find your voice, I promise.

In the pages to follow, you'll find descriptions and prompts to learn and write about your Author Vision, Tone, Audience, Half-Page Summary, and Genre.

LET'S GO.

# BIG WHEELS KEEP ON TURNING
## AUTHOR VISION

OK, before we begin the more concrete portions of a book proposal, I want you to answer the following questions to get your wheels turning. You can write your answers in one line or word, or in paragraphs. By starting to articulate your motivation for this book, it will help as you dive into the other sections. Sometimes people can get discouraged when answering these questions and the doubt can creep in—but don't let it! See this as part of the clarifying process, which is hard but NECESSARY.

So . . .

Why do YOU want to write this book?

What circumstance prompted the idea?

Is it your personal story or experience?

Are you an expert on this topic? (Do you have an audience clamoring for more?)

Is this a creative idea that is original to you?

Why you?

Why now?

Once you have completed those questions, I want you, wherever you are, to say out loud: "I am an author."

## I AM AN AUTHOR!

You just freaked out that old lady on the bus, but I appreciate your enthusiasm.

The author vision is one paragraph and typically in third person. However, some have written as much as a page in first person and pour out their soul. Both work, it just depends on the style of your book and which approach will best explain *what the book will do for the reader.* I recommend third person, and if your author vision is not flowing, try this exercise:

- As quickly as possible, try to make a bullet point list for yourself of all the things you believe the book will do for the reader.

- Pick out the ones you are most passionate about and explain what they are and how you will accomplish them as a writer.

Author vision example for *The Lion, The Witch, and The Wardrobe* by C.S. Lewis:

> Through the magical and enchanting world of Narnia, C.S. Lewis aims to teach children about the themes of good vs. evil, faith, courage, and family. As the Pevensie children enter Narnia and interact with characters such as Mr. Tumnus the Fawn, Mrs. Beaver, and the White Witch, readers are introduced to complex characters who teach lessons about forgiveness, friendship, temptation, and more. Ultimately, Lewis hopes to help his young readers begin to understand the story of Christianity and Jesus through the allegory of life, death, and the resurrection of Aslan the Lion.

While the above example is a made up version for a fiction title, here is a

REAL example from one of my authors, Leah Boden. She is a wonderful Brit[3] like Lewis, with an accent that has made me contemplate calling her to read bedtime stories—to me.

Author Vision example for *Modern Miss Mason: Sharing Charlotte Mason with a New Generation* (forthcoming):

> Charlotte Mason's philosophy, alongside Boden's 21st Century implementation, reminds readers of the power of motherhood. The author's vision for this book is to bring the philosophy of Charlotte Mason to life for a modern audience and future generations. Boden aims to inspire mothers who are current home educators, those who aspire to teach at home in the future, and those who simply want to build deeper connections with their children. Boden desires to share Mason's concepts and insight alongside personal stories and practical tools to help mothers reimagine childhood, education, and motherhood in a way that impacts their families as much as it has transformed her own.

---

3  Until the Oprah and Meghan Markle interview, I was a big self-proclaimed Monarchist. Gotta say, I would still 100 percent do a big bow if I saw Her Majesty in the flesh. Been practicing for years, so it's muscle memory at this point.

*Write your vision for this book and what you hope it will do for the reader.*

[**Pro-Tip**] Print or write out your author vision and dream case scenario and post it in your writing space so you can look at it daily and remember WHY you are doing this!

# THAT ABOUT SUMS IT UP
## HALF-PAGE SUMMARY

Your half-page summary is where a literary agent or publisher gets a short, but informational, glimpse at your book! It's usually one of the first things an agent or publisher will read in your proposal, so it needs to be strong and attention-grabbing. It should be written in a descriptive tone, explaining to readers what they can expect from the story. This is different from your author vision: it's written from a third-person objective point of view. In other words, a neutral, observative, descriptive tone.

It can be awkward to write in the third person, but this is the time for your inner journalist to shine. Imagine yourself in a trenchcoat, standing in the dark evening fog with a microphone in your hand. You're a reporter for the eleven o'clock news and you've got to tell the viewers all about this new book you've stumbled upon. Why you are outside doing literary reporting, I DO NOT KNOW, but just go there with me.

Here's an example of what I imagine Louisa May Alcott's half-page summary of *Little Women* sounding like:

In *Little Women*, renowned author Louisa May Alcott tells the story of four sisters growing up in Massachusetts during the Civil War. With busy imaginations and dreams too big for their small home, readers follow along with each sister as they move from childhood into womanhood under the guidance of their mother, Marmee, and the absence of their father who serves in the War. Meg, the oldest, is wise, kind, and longs for a family of her own.

Jo, the next in line and protagonist of the book, is a tomboy who writes under the cover of moonlight and fights traditional expectations placed on her as she grows into a young woman. Beth, a musician, keeps the peace in her family with her soft spirit and devotion to her sisters. Last but never least, Amy is the spoiled youngest who spends her days painting and dreaming of the finer things her family cannot afford. As the March daughters grow up and face challenges together and apart, Alcott presents different understandings of what it means to dream, love, accept duty, endure heartache, and remain devoted to family. A story that has stood the test of time, readers close the book with an appreciation of childhood, family, and not being afraid to be who you were born to be.

As shown above, the half-page summary gives your readers a glimpse of what the story is about. It doesn't give away *too* much about the detailed storylines, but enough to give the reader an understanding of the plot and book goals. Your summary will look different from other writers, especially if you are writing non-fiction, fiction, self-help, or an autobiography, but accomplishes a similar goal.

Still looking for more examples? Go to Amazon and read the descriptions of some of your favorite books' descriptions. THIS is what you are going for—what will pull the reader in? Additionally, what might they be searching for that would cause them to stumble across your book?

If you self-publish, your half-page summary is the perfect way to write your book's Amazon description! Use those keywords that connect to what people are searching and plug them into your half-page summary and book description.

1. Write a list of as many words and phrases you can think of someone writing that might lead them to your book.

2. Using the above list, write a half page summary of your book in third person.

3. If you're really feeling stuck, try this template:

   a. Briefly describe your book plot in five to seven sentences (See Little Women example, first six sentences.)

   b. Outline your goals as an author (See Little Women example, sentences seven and eight.)

# PLEASE WATCH YOUR TONE, SIR
## TONE

Discussing your tone can be short and sweet. Or less sweet and more so a list of descriptive words that describe how this book will read to your audience. Here are some examples:

Example #1: Story-driven, humorous, travel journal meets therapy session

Example #2: Journalistic, hopeful, analytical

Example #3: Affectionate, inspiring, relatable (described by Louisa May Alcott herself [4])

You might be feeling like this is a tedious thing to do and you might be tempted to skip over it, which of course, you are free to do. But let me come back to what I hear from so many writers, and that is a desire to be confident in their voice as a writer, which comes as a result of processing and clarifying your message. Remember my sorta life story that I shared in the beginning of this book?

*I skipped that too, Joy.*

Go back. I need you to know me. How can we proceed as friends if you don't even care about my life?

---

4   Or, my imaginary L. M. A.

*Do you know anything about mine?*

Touché . . .

But look, the more of these exercises and prompts you can take the time to do now, the stronger your voice, message, and proposal will be, should you choose to keep moving forward with your dream of writing a book.

See, I know about the dreams you've had to write a book. Dreams that you've only told trusted friends. That should count for something, my friend.

*Touché, Joy.*

> **PROMPT**
> ..........
> *Describe your tone as a writer in a short paragraph. Then, try to shave it down to two or three words.*

# SOME STANDING OVATIONS ARE EASIER THAN OTHERS
## PRIMARY AND SECONDARY AUDIENCE

Who are you writing this book for?

It's tempting for us to say, "MY BOOK IS FOR EVERYONE!" The reality is, writing to a wide audience typically makes it harder to focus your message and make your voice clear. The more specific you get, the easier it will be for people interested in your topic to find your book, because you've written it just for them! Those that fall into the category of primary audience will feel much more connected and loyal to your book (and apt to tell their friends about the book or leave a great review) rather than if you had written to the sought after "everyone."

Let's use this book for example. It's about preparing to write a book. Now, there are people who are preparing to write a book who have written best-selling books already. They could potentially benefit from these prompts and insights, but they are not who I have in my mind when I am writing. The people that are in my head as I write this are first-time authors and have been wanting to get their book out into the world for a long time. These people are daunted by book proposals, have never stepped foot in a publisher's office, don't "do" marketing and platform building because it feels "inauthentic," and have no idea where to start for self-publishing.

Does any of that feel like you?

My secondary audience would be people who are less clear on if they really do have a full book in them, and want to use this writing process to see if the idea has legs or "if there's a there, there." Perhaps they have written before but they weren't happy with the success of their book, or they didn't feel like they navigated the publishing or marketing world as well as they could have. They want to do it better this time.

So let's start again, who are you writing for?

*Um . . . everyone.*

No!

*But Joy, there ARE books that everyone ends up reading.*

True, and while I haven't spoken to all the authors of the world, I feel confident in saying that if we did speak to them, they typically had a person or people group in mind as they wrote. And not just non-fiction writers, but fiction too.

And before you resist this idea of focusing your audience more, close your eyes. Imagine your book being held by someone. Who is it?

*No, Joy, I just write for me.*

I thought you wrote for everyone?

*I write as an artistic outlet, but I know my works could apply and touch the world if they would only see how brilliant I am. But I don't really care if anyone else reads my writing.*

You sure?

*Yes.*

Then why do you want to write a book? Why not just journal?

*Are you trying to pick a fight?*

Not at all. I think writing for yourself can be an incredible, creative, and even healing practice. But so many people who want to write a book balk at marketing themselves, their work, or marketing *to* an audience because it feels icky to them. If that's the case, I respect that, but I question why you want your idea to be in book form—published. Look, if your target audience is YOU, then there's part of you that knows there are other people like YOU out there that might enjoy or benefit from what you've written. If you didn't think that on some level, then you'd be satisfied with just journaling, right?

But we don't need to belabor this anymore.

*Good.*

So, if you write for you, then use this prompt to describe yourself. You could even do a creative exercise and make up a fictional reader and describe their life, so as you write, really imagine "Jane."

Here's an example of creating a character to describe your primary audience based on Louisa May Alcott's *Little Women*:

> *Little Women*'s primary audience is Jane, a young adult who enjoys coming-of-age and historical fiction stories. She loves running her weekly book club at a local coffee shop. You can often find her wandering around her neighborhood, taking walks on weekends as she listens to her favorite podcast, *This American Life*. She is currently battling expectations put on her by her family to take

over the family farm (which she loves), but she also has a dream of becoming a famous writer. Her family doesn't know it yet, but she was accepted into a prestigious creative writing program in England and if she accepts, there will be no one to take over the farm.

Here's another example with a more traditional approach:

*Little Women*'s primary audience is women between ages thirteen and thirty who are lovers of historical fiction and stories of sisterhood. The reader is someone who has big dreams and loves to get lost in a story that may be the only voice telling her she can accomplish those dreams. A romantic at heart, the reader identifies strongly with the tension one can feel between love of family, love of a partner, and love of your craft. Can you have them all? This reader will find a book they can talk about with friends, each having a character they call themselves and label their friends. "Of course you're Beth!" "No, I want to be Jo!" "Hate to say it, but she's Amy all the way."

A final example with a concise description:

*Little Women*'s primary audience is young, creative women struggling with identity, expectations put on them, and how to pursue their dreams.

## SECONDARY AUDIENCE

The secondary audience, or sometimes called "extended audience," is the people whom you weren't necessarily writing to as described in your primary audience, but due to the topic and content, they may become interested in your book.

Here are a few ways to think about it . . .

Is your book for teenagers? A secondary audience might be parents who want to peek in and learn more about their kid's interests and way of understanding the world.

Is your book a theology book for people who hold your same faith? A secondary audience might be people who are spiritually unsure, but in a process of learning about different religions.

Is your book a book for CEOs? A secondary audience might be college students who are not currently in that position, but their professors make it assigned reading because of how foundational the principles are for future leaders.

*Describe your secondary audience. These are the readers who you didn't necessarily have in mind when writing, but may, for several different reasons, become interested in your book. This should be in third person and in a similar style to how you described your primary audience a few pages back.*

# THE HORROR, THE HORROR!
## GENRE

This will be easy. Plus, I imagine you might need a break from sitting.

Get up, and wherever you are—your house, coworking space, or The Enchanted Forest—go find a few books and flip them over. Somewhere near the ISBN and long bar code on the back, there should be a genre or genres listed. This helps the book get correctly categorized in a bookstore and online. After looking at a few books and getting an idea for the different types of genres, pick one that best describes your book, or possibly two if you really can't decide.

If the location you are in has no books, I'll give you some examples, but I still think it's a good idea to get up and do a few stretches.

I'll wait.

Back? OK.

Genre Examples:

Fantasy, Children's Literature

Food and Drink

Fiction, Literature

Humor, Gift Books

Biography, Autobiography, Memoir

Travel, Humor

Religion, Christian Life, Spiritual Growth

Health and Wellness

**PROMPT**

*Look at the genres of books similar to yours. They are usually on the back or inside the dust jacket of a book. Write one or two genres that fit your book best.*

# BOOK AT A GLANCE

*WE ARE NOT MESSING AROUND NOW, FOLKS*

Now, we will start to zoom out to look at your book as a whole. Our first step is to organize the overall skeleton of your book: the titling, table of contents, and chapter summaries.

Do I start my book with the heroic retelling of when I rescued a baby dolphin and raised him as my own WHILST being allergic to salt water? Or, do I begin each chapter of my business-how-to book with different U2 lyrics to set the stage for my groundbreaking strategies!?

After that, we will learn about comparable works (*am I more of an Edgar Allan Poe or Brené Brown?*) and then close out the chapter with some logistical prompts that are always important to have in a book proposal, or simply for your own goal setting.

# TO BE CLEAR OR NOT CLEAR, THAT IS THE QUESTION
## WORKING TITLE, SUBTITLE, AND ALTERNATIVE TITLES

When it comes to your title, think about a few phrases that are exciting, intriguing, and clear. Your title should make sense when considering your story, as well as your primary and secondary audiences. Does your title speak to them? Will your audience be able to find your book based on its title?

Titles should also not be overwhelmingly long; however, subtitles are a great way to have fun and pack in more helpful information about your book right on the front cover.

For example, Malcolm Gladwell has a book called *Talking to Strangers*. Based on just the title, it's a little vague what his book will be about. Is it interviews with people he's never met? A recap of awkward encounters on public transportation? A memoir of being stranded alone on an island and getting to know the palm trees he now calls Jennifer, Giles, and Sandy?

However, the full book title is *Talking to Strangers: What We Should Know about the People We Don't Know.* OK—more helpful information! (Although I'm still voting for palm tree memoir.) From this added subtitle, we understand that his book is going to give us insight into how to go about talking to strangers.

When considering what your title and subtitle might be, another important question to ask about your title idea is if it has strong SEO.

*S.E. What?!*

This stands for Search Engine Optimization, which means you have written your content in a way that boosts its place in search engine results, giving people organically searching for something similar to your book's topic a better chance of stumbling across your book. Now, this won't always apply to the genre of book you are writing, but especially if your book is non-fiction, you will definitely want to dedicate some time to evaluating different keywords people search in your genre or topic to potentially incorporate into the title. There are several programs and people who can also help you in this process. Just search, "SEO keywords book titles" or something like that, and a business or blog that has worked hard to put those keywords in *their* title or company tagline to help people searching for information about using SEO for book titles will come up for you.

*It's like SEO inception.*

Exactly.

Here's another example: when I was looking for a literary lawyer, I had asked several lawyer friends if they knew someone who could help me. I got some referrals, but nothing that fit exactly what I wanted. My husband decided to just Google "literary lawyer," and wouldn't you know, my now lawyer for all things literary was the first person to pop up in my search. I love her and couldn't be happier. She wasn't some I.T. expert or SEO maven working the system and paying for Facebook ads, she simply picked a website that clearly stated what I would be looking for and needing. It is LITERALLY just literary-lawyer.com and my husband found her in .037 seconds.

Smart lawyer. Smart husband.

Being searchable doesn't mean your title and subtitle have to be boring, but searchability should be factored in. Self-publishing or not, this is something all the traditional publishers weigh as they finalize titles. The tricky thing is that SEO can be a moving target. Searchability and keywords can also be something that trend. For example, the number of people who were searching for books on Y2K in 1999 is probably *sliiiightly* less now. There are websites where you can enter keywords and see how popular they are right now, but if you don't want to get into the weeds on all of that, simply ask yourself:

*If I was the target reader searching answers to the questions of what my book will do for them, are any of the words they might Google in my title or subtitle?*

Here's another successful SEO example that may or may not be based on my real life. As you would imagine, my kids are perfect cherubs who do no wrong. But, if I were to prepare for the off chance day they ignored my instructions, I might sit down and Google: "~~WHY WON'T MILLIE LISTEN TO ME?!!?~~" "Book on how to get my kids to listen," and do you know what the first book that pops up is titled?

*How to Talk So Kids Will Listen, And Listen So Kids Will Talk* by Adele Faber and Elaine Mazlish.

This book came out in 2002, and I'm sure it's fantastic, but it also has a title that answers the real questions people are asking. Back when you had to go browse a book store, you could pick up as many different books as you wanted to find which you were drawn to, what cover you liked, and if the thickness of the book would make you look smart to the cute cashier upon check-out. Now, analytics and search engines play a big role in what you virtually "pull off the shelf."

*What if my book doesn't fall into a self-help type genre? What if it's fiction?*

Good question. This exercise is still important because finding searchable keywords and phrases will be what you can incorporate into your back cover copy or, if you have an Amazon author page, the book description. Amazon and other sites still use those descriptive paragraphs to pull keywords that people are searching for, so incorporating them as much as possible (without sounding like a robot) is really beneficial.

For now, write down a title that is *your* current favorite. It doesn't have to be what we end up with, but put one title and subtitle as a placeholder. One day, that placeholder might just hit the *New York Times* Best Seller list.

> **PROMPT**
>
> Write out your favorite title and subtitle.

## ALTERNATIVE TITLES AND SUBTITLES

Unfortunately, publishers have strong opinions on titles too, and between their understanding of the market demands and the importance of SEO, they might have other ideas for your beloved title. So, hold it loosely. (But, if it's really important to you, you also can put up a strong argument for why you want to keep it in place.) If you want a stronger chance of being involved in that process, taking some time to brainstorm other options is always a beneficial exercise—plus, it can be an opportunity to test out different titles on your friends, family, and audience to see what they like!

Make this exercise as messy as you want! Write the same title with 472 slightly different variants. Write down the title you think would NEVER make it or feel embarrassed to write down, and just let your brain flow.

*There are no dumb questions and there are no dumb titles, right, Joy?*

I mean, that's subjective, but there's nothing dumb about letting your creative brain freeflow and getting some "dumb" down—it may just lead to the title that makes your publisher say, "THAT! That is the title!"

I recently worked with my business coach on my "Punchline Pillars," which is just an internal document for our team to reference for what we are all about as a company. I was supposed to come to our next meeting with an updated version, and it wasn't quite working, until all of a sudden, the newest version of the pillars came to me . . . IN RHYME.

My coach is very successful, works in an executive level position, and manages 10k employees at one of the largest companies in the world. Big time stuff. Anyways, I was embarrassed to show her my pillars because they sounded like a five-year-old's nursery rhyme. But, with a bit of sweat under my arms, I told her, "I don't know how this happened, but this is what I've got."

Maybe she was just being nice, but she said they were great, and reminded me of what TYPE of company I started and that being quippy and creative with language was right on brand.

I'm not saying your titles should rhyme and be toddler appropriate, but don't let a thought like "this is stupid" keep you from what flows into your head, because one day, that title might get read, or fill you with dread, but just do what I said. OK, Fred?

---

*PROMPT*
...............
*Throw in all the other titles and subtitle ideas that you are considering or tossing around. When you enter them into a proposal, narrow them down to your top three to five extra.*

---

# SETTING THE TABLE MAKES IT EASIER TO EAT
## TABLE OF CONTENTS

As you think about your Table of Contents, try to imagine yourself as someone who doesn't know anything about your book, but has just found it on the shelf of that little corner independent bookstore they love. As they skim your table of contents, or "T.O.C." as they say in the biz, would they be intrigued? Confused? Excited to dive in? How can you edit your T.O.C. to better frame and explain your chapters and book outline?

*But Joy, some of the books I read don't have a T.O.C.*

Yes, but whether or not you have one in your final book, I highly recommend you doing this for yourself as well as for any agent or publisher that might look at your proposal.

> **[Pro Tip]** *Agents and publishers get a lot of proposals on their desk (or in their inbox), and you have a very short window for them to catch your vision and get on board with your book. Having a descriptive table of contents and quick chapter summaries can be the thing that makes them decide if they are going to scroll down and actually give your sample chapters a more in-depth review.*

This prompt will also help you visually see the flow and layout of your book. Here's a less appealing image: the skeleton of your story. You may think you already have the order of your book down, but as you write your table of contents, take another look and see if there might be a better order for your chapters. If you're writing a memoir, is it 100 percent chronological? Why might you *not* want to do that? Why might you? Does the thesis of your book only get introduced in section two of your book? Would putting it in chapter one give away too much or draw a reader in?

In the words of *Reading Rainbow*'s LaVar Burton, "You don't have to take my word for it."

You should have lots of examples of what a T.O.C. looks like lying around your own home. Pick up your favorite books and see how the author organized their content to find inspiration.

The titling of that content can also look different than just "Chapter 1, 2, 3, . . ." Some book's T.O.C. are simply a list of chapters, while others are divided under sections or parts. Note what you see as you skim your books, and if there's any similarities between books of the same genre or not. Did the author title the sections or parts? Do you notice a theme between how chapters are titled?

Then, think about your book and how you could format your T.O.C. in a way that is most fitting with your voice and book. Consider if you want a list of chapters, sections, parts, and if they'll be listed with words, Roman numerals, or images of tiny kittens. If you decide to name your chapters, will it be descriptive and to the point, or do you want to write titles that make people laugh?

In short, your table of contents is an opportunity to intrigue your reader, so the main thing to keep in mind is: if someone from your target readership was to skim your T.O.C., would they be drawn to dive into your book? Let's make this the high dive of all T.O.Cs., shall we?

List your table of contents and potential sections, prologues, etc. here.

# PUBLISHER CLIFFSNOTES
## CHAPTER SUMMARIES

Your chapter summaries are where you are going to want to put in some real elbow grease. Succinctly describing each of these chapters as if you've already written them will be an incredible practice in clarifying your message and getting an idea for the outline of your book, especially if your book isn't completed yet. If you haven't written out the chapters in their entirety yet, putting in the time to write a summary of each chapter will make the writing part fly! (Or, fly at a slightly faster speed than if you were just staring at a blinking cursor on a blank page.)

Looking to the future, as you pitch to publishers, agents, or even engaging your online audience, the more and more you can practice succinctly communicating the direction of each chapter, section, and the book as a whole, the stronger your book will sound. And remember: it's OK if your chapters end up changing a bit, or you move around the T.O.C. order as you continue to write your book. Writing is a process, and the process will bring new ideas and organization to light. However, if you are working on a proposal, you need to have these included, even if they will change.

As an agent, if I can't understand verbally or in written form what the point of each chapter is, and what the author's overall goal is, I lose the ability to see how I, as an agent, could sell their book, and that's my job! I have to be so giddy excited about what you are doing that I want to shout it from the rooftops, and to be excited, I need to clearly know what your book is about. So, as we work on our content, we need to make sure we can hook and engage publishers, agents, or the person searching for their next good read.

One author said to me that they felt like they were giving away too much information in the chapter summaries. To which I responded, "Yes! Give it all away!"

Remember when we talked about the elevator pitch? Another visual I give for the proposal process is to think of it as a waterfall. If you hand someone your proposal and they read your one sentence summary, do they want to learn more? If so, I feel like the current is picking up. If they read your T.O.C., do their eyes move faster to find your chapter summaries? And if they read a chapter summary, are they going to be so interested that they rush to dive in and read your sample chapters?

Trust me, chapter summaries may feel tedious because they ultimately won't go in your book, but they are integral to giving the people viewing your proposal an overview and to working towards the ultimate goal: signing you as an author. Agents and publishers don't have the capacity to read full manuscripts every day, so this proposal is your Niagara Falls. Or maybe it's the barrel you get in to go over the Niagara. Either way, I think you get the analogy.

I do.

The thing I like about this section is writing it in first person. You can tell what you're doing in each chapter *and why* in your own words. Here is an example from my made up *New York Times* Best Seller, *CEO to Farmer Joe: Why I Closed My Laptop, Dropped the Hustle, and Turned to the Amish Way of Living.*

(Please imagine me writing this by hand with a manicured beard.)

### Chapter 1: Life Before Amish

In this chapter, I walk readers through what my life was before I decided to become Amish. I outline my corporate life, working over fifty hours per week in Chicago. I explain how I was making a phenomenal salary as a CEO of a global company with 20k employees underneath me, but evenings were filled with take-out meals, working on the couch, and *The Office* playing in front of me . . . again. One day, after my Chicago O'Hare flight was grounded due to weather, I decided to drive to Detroit to close what I thought was "the deal of a lifetime." As my car was spinning off the country road and into a ditch that Eli and Amos would pull me from hours later, I never imagined I would go on to be rescued from far more than just my car.

> ### PROMPT
> ............
> *You are going to need quite a few pages for this one, but thankfully you've already written your T.O.C., so now all you need to do is plug in a few lines to describe the most intriguing point of each chapter, and how each chapter uniquely contributes to the big idea of your book. Keep the publisher in mind and keep them reading!*

# IT'S OK TO HAVE FAVORITES
## PICKING/WRITING THREE SAMPLE CHAPTERS

Are you ready to start writing, for real? Maybe you want to hop on your computer for your sample chapters but I'd love you to write the first sentence of your book here. Then, one day when you are long gone and people are reminiscing about the greats, they can save up their money, fly to the world famous author museum, and then, pushing through a crowd that only Mona Lisa could contend with, they will get a glimpse of this book behind glass. It will be opened to this page with a tiny plaque that reads,

*"Here lies the hand written words of* _____ YOUR NAME HERE _____ *who*

*penned the first chapters of* _____ YOUR BOOK TITLE HERE _____

*on* _____ TODAY'S DATE HERE _____ *in* _____ YOUR LOCATION HERE _____ .

*Please do not lean on the glass."*

*Ok, but for real, you gave us one week to write the sample chapters. Is that humanly possible?*

Look, I told you on day one to get writing. And I realize this is a lot and you might need to rearrange some of the days and goals to fit your other demands of life, but I did say this book was *slightly aggressive*. Since I have worked with several authors that have hit these goals, my logic is that you've really carved out this month to work hard. You aren't procrastinating and watching Netflix, and you aren't checking Instagram every five minutes.

I know the Instastory ads are so perfectly tailored that you can't help but click "Shop Now" because WHAT HAPPENS WHEN THE STORY GOES AWAY? But trust me, it will still be there tomorrow because your phone and Mark Zuckerberg are always listening.

Many of you are coming to the table with some writing already done, so this will be the time to edit, edit, edit and look at your writing through the lens of the prompts you've done so far. Do your chapters reflect your half-page summary accurately? Did clarifying your audience bring any clarity to your voice as you write?

If you truly have nothing written, this would be the time to try and get away for a few days and write like crazy.

If a writing cabin in the woods isn't at your financial fingertips, there are other ways to get disciplined. For instance, The Pomodoro Technique, developed by a dude named Francesco Cirillo in the 1980s, involves you setting a timer for twenty-five minutes and then taking a short break. After four of these cycles, you take a longer break. The intervals are named "Pomodoros" after the Italian word for tomato, because Cirillo had a tomato shaped timer that he used in college.

*BRB. Running to Bed Bath & Beyond to find one of those timers!*

No! You're procrastinating again. There are several apps that will help make this easier and they are probably cheaper than what you will find at BBB or the cost of an Airbnb. Work as hard as you can this week and know that you are the only one that can make or break your deadlines. If you can't get them done, it's not the end of the world, but if you challenge yourself, make the time, and really try, you'll get far more accomplished than you think you can.

*Do I just write the first three chapters as my sample?*

No, not necessarily. I recommend picking three chapters (and only three, because again, if you are doing a proposal, you need to not overwhelm the person that is taking it into consideration) that give the best overview of your book and range of writing. My friend, Stephanie, who is an acquisitions editor, said she finds the first sentence of a book and the last chapter to have some of the most important pieces. So, if you don't know which three chapters to use for a proposal, I would suggest the first, the last, and something in the middle that really showcases your work.

You ready, da Vinci?

> **PROMPT**
>
> Write your three sample chapters! If you are looking for a way to figure out chapter length, check out the next section. Or, if you don't like math, and you want me to give you a goal to hit, try to write 5k words per chapter. But don't force yourself to write what isn't necessary or limit yourself if it's flowing. You can always go back and edit, or have it edited.

# CARRY THE FOUR, DIVIDE BY SEVEN
## WORD COUNT

Are you ready for one of those loathed story math problems from fourth grade?

**Question:** If the average book page has 275 words per page and your manuscript currently has three chapters and 13,750 words written, how many chapters remaining do you need to hit 55,000 words?

**Answer:** Train B will arrive at Station D at 2:04 p.m.

*Got it.*

Your word count depends on a few different factors, like your genre of book (take this one for example—it's NOT your standard word per page). If you don't have your final word count, giving a word count range is acceptable, and you can find that range by calculating the number of chapters in your table of contents with your average word count per chapter thus far. Unless you are writing a WWII historical tome, a safe bet for a non-fiction, informational type book could be 45-65k words. Memoirs and novels usually run longer and can get up to over 100k. If you have an estimated guess based on the length of one of your chapters, then I recommend writing a range with a buffer of 5k or so on either side of that estimate.

Example for a proposal:

Word Count: 50-60k

# WHAT'S OUR STATUS, FOLKS?
## MANUSCRIPT STATUS AND DELIVERY DATE

In your proposal, it's helpful to give your agent or publisher an idea of where your book's writing stage is. This part is also really simple if you are working on a proposal to a publisher. Either state the number of chapters, words, or percentage of the book you have written at the time you turn in your first draft to a publisher. If it's 100 percent, write "Complete." This doesn't mean it's perfect, but it's at a spot you like enough for an editor or editorial team to dive in on and . . . start tearing apart all your hard work.

Examples:

- 70 percent completed.

- Incomplete. Three sample chapters included.

- To be written.

- Complete.

The delivery date is when you estimate when you will complete the first draft of your manuscript, based on the time from which a contract would be signed. Also, be realistic about your deadline habits! If you are a first-time writer who has to ask for extensions on a writing deadline, you're not starting off on a great foot with the publisher. The phrase I use more than any other in my life and business is: UNDER PROMISE, OVER DELIVER. I would strongly encourage you, if you want to make writing a career, to be professional and have a good reputation in the biz, find a way to DELIVER.

Examples:

- Six months from contract signing.

- Upon contract signing (write this if your book is complete).

- Three to six months from contract signing.

---

**PROMPT**
............
*Write your word count, manuscript status, and delivery date.*

---

# LITERARY MARKETING

*RELATIONAL MARKETING CAN REACH MORE
THAN JUST YOUR MOM*

Most authors would rather be writing than strategizing about endorsements, launch teams, and email lists. Whether you are self-publishing or traditional publishing, marketing is all part of the job if you want anyone besides the Kinko's employee printing out your book to know of your accomplishment.

We live in a time when marketing is mostly left up to the author, and the rules of marketing constantly change with new experts telling us what to do and moving algorithms that haunt our dreams. Before the age of social media, algorithms, and SEO, marketing was far more in the hands of the publisher. Now, marketing can sometimes feel like learning a new language—a language the author is responsible for knowing and where words regularly change in meaning and spelling, but a necessary one to learn if we want people to know about our book.

Throughout this section, you will see examples of the different areas of marketing you can speak to in your proposal, as well as space to brainstorm your answers.

While it often gets a bad rap, not all of marketing is cringe-worthy or daunting. My general advice to authors is to create a marketing plan that feels right to them and focuses on one or two methods that already feel like they have life and momentum behind them. This can make marketing feel authentic, and even enjoyable at times! (Yes, it's possible.)

Authenticity is another word I hear from people all the time regarding marketing, and all I can say is that *only you* will know if you are being authentic or not. Don't let the wondering waste your time. This section will really focus on what feels most authentic and natural to you. To get started, try this proactive and clarifying exercise to find an authentic approach to marketing that fits you:

Who are the people you follow or subscribe to on social media that you don't personally know, but like? How have they made you feel comfortable and engaged? Use these people as a reminder that it is possible to easily encourage and reach people all over the world because of this digital age we live in.

Another question: Do you tend to follow more people or organizations? Most of us follow people, even if the people are telling us about their organization or business, and it's the people who usually feel real to us and tend to have more responsive and engaged audiences.

Now, think of a few areas where you know you can most authentically communicate and invite friends in to join you. Consider different platforms you can use to communicate with an audience, like social media platforms, podcasts, an email newsletter, or any others you can think of. Once you think of one or two ways you would feel comfortable using and sharing, use that platform as a catalyst to let people know about this book you are working on. Yes—you can tell people! They can't know what you don't tell them, and they can't share what they don't know exists! Whether it's just dropping a hint that a book may be in the works, or writing a formal announcement that you're finally doing this thing you've been dreaming of–start to get familiar with engaging your audience, asking them questions, getting feedback, and letting them in on the process.

*That's a little nerve-racking.*

I know, but you gotta *Field of Dreams* it a little. And don't worry—you're not getting off the marketing hook that easy. This is just the beginning of thinking how you will get your book into readers' hands. In this section, we will dive into some specific but critical marketing tactics, and then show how those tactics can be communicated to a publisher in your proposal.

> ### PROMPT
>
> List the people you follow on social media, podcasts, or newsletters that you think, "Hey, I could be friends with them!" Then, list what areas of engagement you feel most comfortable with or feel the most traction with already. (i.e. your own podcast, socials, newsletter, latest hip platform I'm too old to be on, etc.)

# CAN'T LIVE WITHOUT 'EM
## NETWORK AND ENDORSEMENTS

Everyone will approach marketing and their networks in different ways, and that is OK. You can decide how you want to best work with who you know to help spread the word about your book.

*What do you mean by "network," Joy?*

I mean, your network is the people and organizations you either have a strong personal relationship with, or even just a connection, and might be interested in a partnership, giveaway, or cross promotion. The more you have genuinely cheered others on or worked to create partnerships, the increased probability that people will want to get the word out about your work.

Your network is also seen by publishers as a reflection of the audience you are trying to reach through your writing, so if you have a strong core group of people who are ready to talk up your book, the other readers that don't know about you yet are likely to find your work. Including this in your proposal helps sales and marketing teams best calculate and strategize.

Don't assume publishers will just know your network, and remember that this is a section of your proposal the publishing house sales team will review to assess the type of investment (advance) they can make from a safe and calculated position, all based on how many copies they think your network can help sell. If that feels icky to you, remember that the house is a business, and can only stay in business if they are strategic in who they publish. It might also help to view your network as your collection of cheerleaders who will be happy to do what they can to get your book out there.

We can't really blame publishers for needing this information, especially since so many people shop online. You can think of your "network" as . . . hmmmm, let's call them, "Janet." You've just opened the door to the bookstore, and the sound of tiny bells, tied to the top of the door, jingle behind you as it closes. The noise alerts "Janet" that a customer has arrived. You want to buy a new book, but don't have anything in particular in mind. "Janet" lets you know that she's just read the best book and would highly recommend you check it out. So, you do! You like Janet, and you trust her recommendation because you've been ~~following her on social media~~, coming to this bookstore for years.

Is this analogy getting annoying? I think you get it. Your network should be a list of "Janets" for your potential readers—people and organizations who hold credibility to their followers, who will recommend your book, and tell people how to buy!

How might this look in your proposal? Here are some examples:

 **List your network and their reach:**

- Sally Smith (personal friend): 15k on Instagram @sallysmith-fakeinsta, 5k weekly podcast listeners on "Sally Smith has a Fake Podcast" and 25k friends on Facebook.com/sallysmithfakeface-book.

- Sally Jones (colleague): 18k on Instagram @sallyjonesfakeinsta, 10k YouTube subscribers and an ongoing column in *Vogue Magazine*.

**Or, write about your network in first person:**

- I am part of a network of over 1,500 entrepreneurs who are dedicated to promoting and encouraging one another's work. So far within our group, fifty of the members have written books, and forty of them have hit #1 in their Amazon category based on our community's support.

- I have ongoing relationships with and appeared previously on the following networks and podcasts including: *Fake Podcast Today, Fake News Today, Fake Radio Program Today.* (Include non-fake hyperlinks if sending a proposal digitally.)

- I have ongoing relationships with the following influencers: Sally Smith (Combined reach of 100k+), Sally Jones (Combined reach of 150k+).

Then, it's time to come to the table with endorsements. You may think of an endorsement as that one-to-two sentence comment of praise you often see on book covers, or sometimes listed within the first few pages of a book. However, this type of marketing has also changed, and we are no longer bound to just written endorsements. If you are going to ask someone to endorse you, we want to be strategic about what kind of endorsement you are getting from that person. It's fine if you list only the names of your endorsers, but remember that a *written* endorsement is not always the only option anymore—endorsements can include videos, interviews, social media posts, etc.

You'll want to have endorsements divided into these three categories in your proposal, and you can show that you are thinking strategically by describing the type of endorsement they will give.

**See examples below:**

### Confirmed Endorsements: (Shoot for about ten)

- Sally Smith: Written endorsement and thirty-second video endorsement.

- Sally Jones: Instagram Live interview and pre-order push.

- John Doe: Written endorsement and social media endorsement.

- John Smith: Social media endorsement and Instagram Live interview.

### Potential Endorsements:

- Heather Hypothetical: CEO of A Big Company.

- Phil Fakerton: Cousin of neighbor and Tik Tok star with 3 million followers. Has said yes to reading my sample chapters.

- Moira Madeupter: College roommate and founder of The Non Profit You've All Heard Of.

### Dream Endorsements:

- Reese Witherspoon

- Oprah

- Edgar Allan Poe (Might be tough)

Brainstorm people and organizations in your network who could endorse your book, how you will reach out, and when and/or who you might need to reach out to and ask for them to make an introduction . . . to Reese.

# WHO'S YOUR OPRAH?
## FOREWORD

Not all books have forewords, but if the other books in your genre do, I would strongly recommend including this in a proposal. A foreword can really make a difference with a publisher because this person's name can be listed on the cover or in the book description online. The person you want to write your foreword is typically someone who is a known author or influencer, because if you are a first-time writer, that known person is giving you a stamp of approval. They are the FDA to your new vaccine. In your proposal, you can write if they are confirmed or unconfirmed for writing your foreword next to their name.

*But Joy, I don't know anyone famous!*

OK, so maybe Oprah won't agree to write the foreword, and if the person you want isn't someone you personally know and will say YES because they already know and like your writing, then you'll want to make sure you have most of the prompts in this book finished. The reason is, you'll want to thoughtfully pick the best (and edited) content that will win them over.

For example, is your half-page summary perfection? Send that and your T.O.C. with an offer to also send a sample chapter if they are interested to learn more. (Which is why your sample chapter should be in a great place.) Or, have you gotten a confirmed endorsement from someone they also know and respect? Mention their name for credibility, or better yet, ask that person to connect you two. Perhaps they are also a podcaster like you—share with them about your podcast and the listenership or guests you've had that are significant. They might feel connected by this shared experience and want to support a fellow podcaster.

If it feels like bragging to you, and bragging feels gross, remember that **they don't know you**. You aren't bragging, but rather giving information so a stranger can draw a conclusion about your credibility vs. creepiness.

Treat your dream foreword author the same way you would a publisher or agent. Put your best foot (and writing) forward, and don't be afraid to make the ask. You would be surprised how reaching out to people you genuinely admire, whose own writing or work aligns with yours, can often lead to one person (out of, maybe, ten requests) saying yes to your request, *if* you ask the right way.

*How do I ask?*

TELL them how much you've appreciated their writing or impact in the world, and send them a little snapshot of you. (Like the examples I laid out a couple paragraphs back.) Let them know how much it would mean to you to have them consider writing the foreword or give an endorsement. I would ask for both, so that if they can't write the foreword, you might still get an endorsement.

*But, I don't have their email.*

Do they have a website and a contact page? Do you follow each other on social media? Can you send them a kind (non-creepy) video message?

They can't say yes if you don't ask!

PROMPT
...........
Brainstorm your dream foreword writers in the space below or if you have a confirmed Oprah, write it down and make it official! If you want a foreword but need to move forward with your proposal, you can also insert: TBD. Not as eye catching, but works.

Foreword written by:_____

# WHAT'S THE PLAN, STAN?
## MARKETING PLAN AND BOOK LAUNCH

Your marketing plan and book launch is where you lay out your plan to market your book for your potential agent and publisher. This might be something that you find a trusted fellow writer or experienced marketing guru to consult with. The more ideas we kick around together, the better! Think about what you've seen other authors do when marketing their book that you liked, and didn't like. For what you didn't like, ask yourself, "Why?" Was it annoying, but still effective? Did it seem inauthentic? Then, think about an author who marketed their book strongly and effectively. What did you like? Why? What about their tactics caught your interest? What methods have you noticed are common for authors who write in your genre?

If you have a friend who is a published author, reach out to them and ask: what is one marketing tactic you used that was surprisingly effective?

When determining your own marketing plan, the most important thing is to figure out what works best for you, and how *you* want to market. While others can give helpful insight into what worked for them, prioritize what you think will be enjoyable and authentic to you. For example, social media marketing and influencing might come to mind first as a way to market, but is certainly not the only way to market yourself or your project.

Personally, I love relational marketing. Relational marketing means you utilize friends and other people in the industry who will advocate your work for you.

*[Pro Tip] You always increase your chances of people saying yes to this if you are also willing to promote their projects and return the favor!*

You don't have to use every platform to market well (and I recommend you don't), but like I said before, find what areas seem most energizing or have the most current momentum, and focus your efforts there.

Here's a few marketing ideas to kick this off:

**Social Media:** Currently, doing an Instagram Live with another person is a great way to gain traction for a new audience, though social media tactics like this often change. The person you do the Live with should have a decent following (1k-100k followers). Both of you will invite your following to your Live and talk together, discussing your book and getting viewers excited about your work!

**Influencers:** I know we all think that someone with a million followers is going to be more influential than someone with 15k, but the reality is that people with 1k-100k followers are called "micro influencers" and are often more listened to by their followers than people with one million, because they feel more accessible. One of my Punchline Speakers, Liz Forkin Bohannon,[5] had an Instagram following of 25k followers, and interviewed Matthew McConaughey on her podcast called *Plucking Up*. His publicist obviously thought that to promote his book, a podcast host with less than 30k followers on social media would have great impact. And it did! People on her feed went bonkers and shared about it like crazy because it was their *friend*, Liz (who many have never actually met in person), interviewing a celebrity they loved. The show got their attention, and they felt more connected than they might have if the interview was hosted by someone you might *expect* to interview a huge movie star like Mr. McConaughey. So, her listeners shared.

*Alright, alright, alright.*

Are you quoting Matthew McConaughey?

*Yes.*

Well played, friend.

**Email Lists:** These are still the most effective way to turn the promotion of a book into a sale. If you don't have an email list yet, a great way to start is finding someone or several people to do a giveaway with you in order to capture email addresses. (Try using kingsumo.com to launch your email campaign). You can also ask others to promote your book on their email list. I promise—it's going to be a WIN.

**Endorsements:** Remember, endorsements were known as those quotes on the back or opening pages written by notable authors or speakers, but can also come in the form of a social media post or short video. Shoot for asking twenty to fifty people for endorsements and plan to give them the following:

---

5   She was also one of my bridesmaids and did a musical montage at my wedding reception . . . eight months pregnant. That's love.

- One or two sample chapters from your book (with the option to get an advanced digital copy if they want the whole work).

- Ideas for the type of endorsements you are looking for. People can personalize of course, but it's always helpful to have a prompt and idea of the length of endorsement you're looking for (two to four sentences; a three to five sentence paragraph, draft of an email they can send to their audience with images, links at the ready, etc).

**Publicist / PR:** Traditional publishers will hopefully have or contract a publicist to work with you on your book, but I also know traditionally published authors who still hire their own publicist to help with additional connections. Like a literary agent, you want to find a publicist who focuses on your type of literary connections and has an established network of authors who will share your book on podcasts, radio stations, featured spots in magazines, etc. A good way to find the right publicist fit for you is to check out authors you like and see if you can figure out who they work with.

OK. After brainstorming and dreaming about your marketing methods, dream endorsements, and network, you'll want to lay it out clearly and express the personal innovations or marketing investments you are willing to bring to the table in your proposal. This is usually organized as a timeline outlining your marketing plan from months prior to the launch of your book, all the way to the year after your book comes out.

*Really, Joy?*

Not everything will actually be done, but the more you can write down, the more momentum you will feel. On top of that, a publisher will see that you understand their business and what it takes to get a book into the world and that will be very appealing to them.

# PRE-LAUNCH

Take those dream endorsements, network, and marketing methods you brainstormed above, and input them as listed strategies or outlets you can use during the year leading up to the book launch. Insert your name for "Author."

Examples:

- Author will personally promote and bring attention to the excitement of their upcoming book launch.

- Author will secure endorsements from a minimum of fifteen people.

- Author will secure foreword (in collaboration with Publisher's approval).

- Author will create _____# promotional videos about the book.

- Author will pursue the following collaborations to bring ongoing attention:

    - Podcast with_____: Listenership of _____.
    - Podcast with _____: Listenership of _____.
    - IG LIVE with  Viewership of _____.
    - IG LIVE with _____: Viewership of _____.

- Author will write _____# of blog posts related to the book.

- Author will write _____# of social media posts (describe your approach).

- Author will submit articles to the publishing house publicist for any suggested outlets or reach out personally to:

    - Name of magazines.
    - Name of websites.

- Author will connect with _____# of influencers for giveaways (list influencers and their number of followers).

- Author will promote pre-order giveaways.

- Author will promote incentives for launch team.

- Author will . . .

<br>

*PROMPT*

*Brainstorm and list your ideas and abilities for marketing DURING the six to twelve months prior to launching your book.*

# DURING LAUNCH

List strategies or outlets you can execute zero to two months before launch. Get as specific as possible.

 Examples:

- (Feasible) Book tour plans including in-person and virtual approaches.

- Virtual book readings.

- In collaboration with Publisher, Author will send personalized gifts for pre-orders.

- Author will personally engage a Launch Team and equip them with tools to promote the book.

- Author will take as many interviews as Publisher books.

- Author will be available to record a promotional book trailer.

- Author will create a #hashtag for the book, if applicable.

- Author will execute all of the booked IG/FB Lives, Podcast interviews, etc.

- Author will collaborate with the Publisher on a book launch party and think strategically of how to engage as many in-person and online viewers as possible.

Brainstorm your ideas and abilities for marketing the launch of your book.

## POST-LAUNCH

List what strategies you will execute for the year following release.

Examples:

- Ongoing marketing and collaborations online and in person to promote the book.

- Podcast launch (only do this if you really have the bandwidth and desire).

- Speaking at _____, _____, and _____ on the book's central message.

- Collaborate with Publisher and Speaking Agency to get bulk rate orders to event hosts.

- Creation of an online book club (hosted by Author or an outline to give to book club hosts and a willingness to join for each book club's last meeting).

- Private Facebook group for people who have purchased the book.

> **PROMPT**
> ...........
> Brainstorm your ideas and abilities for marketing the book subsequent to your book launch.

# MARKETING YOURSELF

*YOU'RE MORE THAN JUST A PRETTY FACE*

Unfortunately (or fortunately, depending on your personality type and if your dream Saturday involves a live stream of people weighing in on what you should eat for breakfast), being an author today is so much more than being a skilled writer. Traditionally published or self-published, you probably know by now that to get on the radar of readers, you need more than your local bookshop to spread the word. Newly successful writers have often found a way to connect with a community of people who believe in them and are clamoring for more work.

What I find, though, is that many authors resist the idea of marketing themselves or their work because they have public figures in mind who annoy them. Think of those people, write down why they annoy you, and get it out of your system.

# UGH, THE "P" WORD

## ONLINE PRESENCE AND INFLUENCE, AKA PLATFORM

Let's talk about the beast: social media marketing and influence. While this may come naturally to some, and you may already have somewhat of a platform, this can be really intimidating and unfamiliar to others.

One publisher I spoke to said that the growth of an author's platform can be more intriguing than the actual size. For example, someone might have 100k followers, but have they had that same number for a few years? Publishers might be more interested in someone whose platform has grown by 50k in the past six months alone.

I encourage people, if they are just starting to build a platform, to find one avenue of communication (social media, email newsletter, podcast) that they are most energized by and put their focus there. If you have a podcast that is increasing every month by 25 percent listenership, then that means people are sharing your content and something is resonating. However, if you enjoy Instagram and have found a rhythm on that platform that works for you, focus on growing there.

But, don't forget to ask people to share, subscribe, or like. I know it can seem annoying, but really, if you stop and think about the people you listen to or follow that you genuinely like, when they make an ask of you, are you super annoyed? If being annoying is a concern of yours, I can safely say that you probably won't be. Ask tactfully and genuinely using language like:

> "If this material was helpful to you, it would really help me if you could share with a friend, subscribe, and leave a review; or, if you didn't like it, email me—I welcome the feedback. Thanks so much!"

Was that annoying? Nope. Because the reality is, most people, even your biggest fans, may not take these actions if they aren't prompted to do so. If you finish listening to a podcast, do you think, "Hmm, I wonder what action I could take that would ultimately help this person's analytics to lead to them having a greater platform so that a publishing team would be able to see their growth and publish the book I didn't know they wanted to write?" Probably not. However, when your favorite podcast host ends the show with an explanation that leaving reviews really helps her show, sponsorship, and visibility, you might be more apt to take a few seconds to do so!

Lastly, remember in the last section when we talked about relationships? Keep that the focus as you build, and you will feel free in your platform planning. One of our Punchline Speakers, Hannah Brencher, tells people to shift their mindset "from ME to WE."

You should also find comfort in knowing that you can't do all the things, and a platform doesn't always mean social media—it could be your weekly newsletter, online courses, a podcast, or any area that invites others in that grows awareness of your work. When you think of what areas you are going to focus on, think of the WE. Invite others into your work, ask their opinions, honor others, and don't be afraid to give a lot of your content away. While you may be tempted to save it for the book, it actually builds the momentum and excitement around your project.

I have one author who is also a painter and illustrator. He shares probably 80 percent of the content from his books on social media, and when the book comes out, people go crazy and buy it because they have already been convinced they love his work . . . AND love him.

Here's an idea: think about how much you love writing and the stories and messages you want to share with the world. Take that love for writing and think about loving others through your work. If you can find the avenues you enjoy, and communicate and serve others authentically there, that icky "p" word will start to grow. Not overnight, and maybe not to Kardashian levels, but you won't fear the idea of a platform as much. Instead of using it to make yourself superior to others, you are inviting others into your passion and fun.

> **PROMPT**
> ...........
> *What's enough influence for you? How many people do you want to reach with your book?*

# FROM THE PAGE TO THE STAGE
## WRITING AND SPEAKING

If you have accomplishments as a writer or speaker, you will list your accomplishments in this part of the proposal. If you want to include a short paragraph about your history with writing or speaking before each list, I've given an example of that as well. I've included a suggested format to get your ideas going, but make it your own. You can write in first or third person, and remember, if you don't have anything to list, no worries!

## WRITING

I have written both professionally and personally for _____ years. Some of my most notable projects have been _____, _____, and _____. The reason I feel connected to writing is because _____ and my style resonates with people because _____.

PAST WRITING PROJECTS:

- List
- Them
- Like
- This
- And
- If
- Significant
- Include
- Reader
- Numbers

UPCOMING WRITING PROJECTS:

- List
- Them
- Like
- This
- Unless
- There
- Aren't
- Enough
- On
- The
- Horizon
- Then
- You
- Can
- Skip
- The
- Lists
- Altogether

*PROMPT*

*Write about your past and present accomplishments as a writer and your connection to the craft.*

## SPEAKING

I have loved speaking ever since I was twelve years old and joined my middle school debate team. Now as a thirty-eight-year-old, my stage time is less debate and more encouragement. I am typically invited to speak at conferences and on panels addressing the topics of _____, _____, and _____. Over the last few years, I have spoken in person to more than _____ people.

PAST SPEAKING ENGAGEMENTS:

- List
- Them
- Like
- This
- And
- If
- Significant
- Include
- Audience
- Number

UPCOMING SPEAKING ENGAGEMENTS:

- List
- Them
- Like
- This
- And
- Include
- Dates
- And
- Hyperlinks

**PROMPT**

Write about your past and present accomplishments as a speaker and your connection to the craft.

# THIRD-PERSON PROBLEMS
## AUTHOR BIO

If you have been writing for a while, you may already have written an author bio in the past. If so, all you need to do is copy and paste that here! If you're writing it from scratch or reviewing your current bio, I recommend the following criteria:

- Written in third person.

- Average length: 150-300 words.

- Reads as a highlight reel of your professional accomplishments and credibility.

- Includes a few personal anecdotes about family, where you live, or a fun fact.

> **PROMPT**
>
> Write your author bio below. And remember, you ARE an author, even if your book isn't published yet.

# IMITATION IS THE BEST FORM OF FLATTERY
## COMPARABLE WORKS

Remember when I told you to pick up the books around your house and check out their table of contents, or what I sometimes call, "book skeleton"? If you came across a book that reminded you of your own book, it might be one of your comparable works. Comparable works are important to include in your proposal because they give a quick reference point for the person reviewing your proposal to say, "Oh, OK, I'm familiar with that book and can get a clearer picture of where this author is headed." For that reason, it's important to try and find books that are widely known to include in your "CW." However, if your book is about some new insight around Quantum Gravity's String Theory, you might find yourself highlighting some lesser known publications to show that your new angle has been minimally covered . . . UNTIL NOW.

The tension (I use that word because I still have string theory on the brain) for this section will be describing the comparable works while also highlighting why yours is different and still necessary. If your comparable works show that what you want to write about already has ten *New York Times* Best Sellers specifically on your topic, this will also help you figure out if you need to add a new angle, insight, or take that hasn't been said before.

Here is an example of how I imagine Suzanne Collins, author of the totally mellow YA fiction series *The Hunger Games,* would have presented her comparable works:

*Matched* by Ally Condie (Dutton Books for Young Readers, 2010)

Both books focus on a female protagonist in a future, dystopian world. *Matched* follows the story of Cassia, an obedient girl who trusts and lives her life according to whatever the society suggests, while Katniss from *The Hunger Games* shies away from romance and throws herself into a life-or-death scenario to protect her family.

*Divergent* by Veronica Roth (Katherine Tegen Books, 2014)

Roth's storyline centers on a dystopian society that divides its citizens into factions based on an aptitude test. The core difference is that Roth's book follows one girl as she enters a faction at the brink of a war they face together, while *The Hunger Games* centers on a cruel game where everyone is an enemy.

*The Maze Runner* by James Dashner (Delacorte Press, 2009)

Both books feature characters who are thrust into a danger-
ous game or test, building relationships and learning how to out-
think the enemy in order to survive. *The Maze Runner* focuses on a
group of kids trying to survive the Maze while not knowing why or
how they got there, while *The Hunger Games* citizens understand
the world of Panem and the tradition of the Games, and what the
exact implications of the event are.

> **PROMPT**
>
> List three to five comparable titles, their author, imprint, and year published. Describe
> the book in two sentences with a third sentence about how your book is different.

# FRIENDS WITH BENEFITS
## READER BENEFITS

This part is short and sweet. Third person. One to two sentences describing the benefits your readers will have after reading your book.

Here are a few examples that should give you an idea of how to write this (both methods of formatting are acceptable):

*The Great Gatsby* by F. Scott Fitzgerald

**Reader Benefits:** Experience the lifestyle of wealthy New Yorkers during the Prohibition Era, uncover unique symbolism and hidden metaphors in a book packed with underlying themes, closely explore a "rags to riches" story and the benefits and downfalls to expecting money to solve your problems.

*The 7 Habits of Highly Effective People* by Stephen R. Covey

**Reader Benefits:** Readers will (1) learn how to take initiative, (2) identify values, priorities, and principles and apply them to achieve a balanced life, and (3) improve communication to be effective in their personal and professional life.

Write a short description of what your readers will get out of your book. (Besides the surprise $100 bill you are hiding in the dust jacket of every 100th copy. OK, MONEYBAGS, WE GET IT!)

# HAVE I GOT A DEAL FOR YOU!!!
## KEY SELLING POINTS

Are you ready to put your used car salesperson hat on? At car lots, the sales members are told to never let the person looking at a car leave the lot empty-handed. The reason is quite simple—if you can't hook them with a reason to stay and buy from you, there's a million other car lots they could visit and buy from. Tell them you have what they are looking for. KEEP THEM ON THAT CRACKING ASPHALT OR YOU DON'T GET YOUR QUARTERLY BONUS, NED!

So, really, why should they buy YOUR car?

*My name is not Ned. And I'm not selling a car.*

Sorry, it just felt right. But let *me* be Ned for a moment and mansplain the analogy of selling used cars for your proposal's key selling points that you probably already get . . .

Each publishing house has a sales team. If your used car is actually a book, what might a sales team tell a bookstore or buyer to get them to pre-order a bazillion of your ~~car?~~ book? And, if you can't tell a sales team what to say, how will they sell it?

For this section, give as many unique reasons for why and how your book is marketable and will stand out to a publishing house's sales team. Create an eye-catching list, or "key selling points" to help make their job easier and get them to say, "YES! I will buy!"

See, you may get your proposal to one acquiring editor who is very excited about your book, but then they have to get their whole team to sign off on it too. After their team does backflips and gets pumped about your project, *then* it typically goes to the sales team for approval. If an editor foresees that their sales team is going to have a tough time doing their job, they might not greenlight it to pass on to the sales team because they don't want to get a "no."

These are just some of the hoops your potential publishing house needs to go through before they can buy your book. So, if you are able to imagine yourself being on the car lot with a potential buyer who is about to walk over to Dale's Discount Dodgeville, what would you tell them with a smile and a wink as you hand them a day-old donut and stale coffee to sweeten the pitch?

Here are some examples of how you can phrase your key selling points:

- By partnering with _____, this book will reach _____.

- Combining ____ and ____ has never been done before!

- No one is talking about _____!

- This is not a flash in the pan book. It's going to be the topic of discussion because _____.

- This is going to change the universe as we know it!

Now, go read your list to someone in your house (with your most convincing sales voice) and see if they would buy your car, or at least take that stale, half-eaten donut off your hands.

PROMPT

*Write a list or paragraph of key selling points that make your book stand out.*

*DAY 26*

# STRUCTURE, DESIGN, AND EXTRAS

*THAT'S NOT A BOOK, THIS IS A BOOK.*

Some of you will follow a typical format for your book. You will clearly be the voice, the content will be straightforward, and the book will come in a standard form with cover, black and white words, and a barcode on the back.

*Is that OK, Joy?*

Yes! Of course!

However, if you have elements of your book that might be unique or helpful to the person reading your proposal (or listening to your pitch on the elevator), the following aspects are important to think through and articulate clearly—and be realistic about feasibility and cost.

If any of the following three sections spur an idea, write them down, and be sure to include them in your proposal or pitch.

# WHAT IS TIME, REALLY?
## STRUCTURE

Some authors structure their relaying of the information or timeline in a less than straightforward way. Getting creative can make the reading experience confusing (if done poorly), or unforgettable as it captivates the reader's brain and actively engages the content in a new way. For example, you may have heard of *The Book Thief* by Markus Zusak. One of the most unique aspects of the book is that it's narrated not by a character, but by Death. Another example is *The Time Traveler's Wife* by Audrey Niffenegger. This book doesn't read chronologically, or even really have a pattern to the chapters, but bounces around moments during the featured couple's past, future, and present. These are examples of unique structures that you want to mention in the structure section, if applicable.

> *PROMPT*
> ............
> *Do you plan to write your book in a unique structure? Explain it here.*

# ICE, ICE, PAGES
## DESIGN AND SPECIAL FEATURES

Design and special features relate to the physical aspects of your book. Consider a new version of Ray Bradbury's *Fahrenheit 451*, which had a cover that looked like a matchbook. Given it was only used as a creative display (thanks, Fire Marshall), it was also done as a nod to the 200 copies published in the 1950s, which had covers made out of fireproof asbestos. As you can see, sometimes the design elements are done for marketing purposes and can't be rolled out for every copy. I would encourage you, even if you have a great idea for a 3D pop-out musical memoir, to think realistically about a publisher's production budget. Not that you can't propose your really unique hardback, full-color photography that you have to license from Annie Leibovitz, but make sure you are realistic in how you present your production demands. If you can't hold your hopes and dreams loosely, self-publishing might be the best route for your *Tour de Penguins,* printed on pages made of ice and can only be read in a walk-in refrigerator (or the Antarctic) with a robot turning the pages that would otherwise melt upon contact with human hands.

(Note: Amazon delivery is not available for this product.)

OK, more realistically, let's say you are writing a travel guide about your hometown. A special feature might be the old map that was hand-drawn by your great-great-grandfather that you want to include in the back. That is definitely worth mentioning.

Another special feature I love is when authors include childhood photos in the middle of their memoir. I'm a SUCKER for a good awkward childhood photo. And if the captions make me giggle? Even better.

If you have design or special feature ideas, don't do more than three. One is ideal, because it shows you're creative. More than three shows a publisher you don't have a grasp on production costs, and the idea of having to tell you, "no we can't do that," will be daunting to them.

If nothing is coming to mind, don't force it.

You can write this section in first person, third person, or bullet points, depending on what you want to communicate.

# WHAT *FROZEN* DID TO . . . EVERYTHING
## AUXILIARY PRODUCTS

My two-year-old daughter has not seen any of the *Frozen* empire films. And yet, if we are in the store and she sees something with *Frozen* characters, she *still* walks like a newly woken zombie over to those captivating Disney eyes and looks straight into their souls.

I call it the *Frozen* empire because it's so much more than a movie. This franchise found a way to touch every corner of the earth and plant it's branded flag on everything from diapers, to playhouses, William Sonoma's Olaf Cookie Jar, or Zale's $7,000 Elsa engagement ring. I mean, I guess I assumed it was an engagement ring but I wouldn't be surprised if there was some *Richie Rich* seven-year-old out there who demanded her daddy get it for her.

"Daddy I want an Elsa diamond NOW!!"

Before you get diamonds involved, think through your book, and if there are any possible supplemental products that could be sold separately, what might they be? Some examples might be:

- Online masterclass
- Book club discussion guide
- A journal
- Interactive app for daily readings and activities
- ~~Diamonds~~

**PROMPT**

What extras might be produced to sell with or after your book becomes a best seller?

# ASSEMBLING A PROPOSAL

*"DID YOU SEE THAT?!?"*
*-AGENTS AND PUBLISHERS HEARD AROUND*
*THE WORLD*

Every literary agent and publisher has different requirements or availability. Before you find the first contact@whateverwebsite.com address you can find and send them your entire manuscript, first make sure you do the following for literary agents you are interested in working with:

- **Locate** their submissions page. Are they accepting submissions? If they are, do they represent or publish your genre?

- **How** do they want you to contact them? (Side note: I don't recommend reaching out to any professional by messaging them on any social platform. Mayyyyyybe LinkedIn, but the best way to go is through their website.)

- **What** do they want you to submit? Do you have the materials they want prepared?

But wait, wait. Before you close this book and start submitting away, I have some final prompts that will be the icing on the cake, or the . . .

# CHERRY ON TOP
## ONE SENTENCE SUMMARY

When I'm working with authors, I always like to save the one sentence summary for last. This is the very first part of your proposal, and I see it as the most crucial element, the cherry on top, or even the first domino.

*Domino?*

Yes (and I know I've hit this point a million times). Agents and publishers see a lot of proposals. They need to be hooked, enticed, or pushed forward to keep reading the rest of the proposal. Ask yourself:

Would this one-sentence summary compel someone who knows nothing about me or my book to read the half-page summary? Would the half-page summary compel that person to read the table of contents or chapter summaries? WOULD THE CHAPTER SUMMARIES COMPEL THEM TO READ A SAMPLE CHAPTER?

If you've been able to get the proposal in someone's hands, or just trapped them in the corner at a party, would those initial summaries lead them to read your actual, fully written chapters? Would they sip their sangria and tell Bill to turn down the Harry Conick Jr. jams so they could hear more about your book?

This is the sentence of all sentences. No pressure.

*[SILENCE]*

That *was* a lot of pressure, so here's a couple examples to help:

*Harry Potter and the Sorcerer's Stone* brings readers into the magical, adventurous, and sometimes scary world of a young orphan boy, Harry Potter, who realizes he is a wizard, and leaves his abusive aunt and uncle to begin boarding school at The Hogwarts School of Witchcraft and Wizardry, where he makes friends and enemies, and learns just how much power he has.

*Good to Great: Why Some Companies Make the Leap and Others Don't* shows through research what makes companies stop settling for just being "good," and instead transition into companies with superior longevity and performance through defining and teaching key characteristics that make a company great.

# LET'S GIVE 'EM SOMETHING TO TALK ABOUT
## ORDER OF YOUR PROPOSAL

As I mentioned before, each agent and publishing house will have different requirements for what they want you to submit, and even what to specifically put in a proposal. Even though the publishing industry is constantly changing (it's the Publishing Wild West, I tell ya), I guarantee everything you've done so far throughout this book will have you 99.9 percent covered and ready to submit a proposal, which is required by most publishers and, if done well, gets you noticed by agents. You just need to type it up, organize it, and make it look pretty!

[*Teenie Weenie Request*] *If you want the full list of how I have authors I work with organize their proposals, I would be happy to send you the Punchline Proposal format. (I just have one teenie-weenie ask.) Could you leave a review of this book on Amazon, or share about it on Instagram and tag @joyegger-ichs and @punchlineagency so we know what you thought and help us get the word out? That would mean the world! Then, write me an email at authors@ punchlineagency.com, and I will send you a downloadable PDF list of how I suggest ordering your proposal, plus some of my preferred fonts and additional tips for getting your proposal into the world. Let's be honest, I'll send it to you regardless, but a review or share on the socials would make my day!*

# DEV-A-WHAT?!?
## EDITS AND TYPESETTING

Do you want to increase your chances of getting noticed? Make sure you have at least one, if not a few, editors look over your proposal. Here is what I recommend:

1. **Dev Edits:** This is the biz language for the work done by a developmental editor. This type of editor is skilled at looking at the structure, organization, and development of the book. Think big picture. This is what they work on.

2. **Copy Edits:** This is the biz language for . . . well, that's just what it's called. A copy editor will look at your sentences, tone, and style to ensure your words and copy flow well. Yes, even the best writers need an editor.

3. **Proofreading:** This type of editing ensures a final once over for any and all errors. Think dotting the i's and crossing the t's,

except we hope your computer has done that. The main job of a proofreader will be to look for any other grammatical or formatting inconsistencies.

4. **Typesetting:** This is not a must, but it's aesthetically pleasing and shows any agent or publisher that you take your proposal seriously. This is typically not an editor, but someone who works in design and can make your proposal look like it would in the layout of a book. Word, Adobe, and other programs have capability of doing this, so if you like to figure things out yourself, you might not need to hire someone!

If you don't know editors or typesetters, I have several people I work with whom I would be happy to recommend. Email authors@punchlineagency. com and let me know what you need. Remember, we're friends, and I'm here to help, even after this book is over.

# PUBLISHING NEXT STEPS

*MOTHER PENGUIN OR DADDY BEZOS?*

*To be honest, Joy, I've always dreamed of being published with the little orange and black Penguin on the spine of my book.*

That's a good dream. And it very well might be a reality, too! First, let me reiterate that I think the publishing industry is a little like the Wild Wild West right now. A brief lesson, if you will (which very well might have changed by the time you read this book):

## THE BIG FIVE

There are five primary imprints known as "The Big Five" (and used to be the big six, but I think you can see what happened) who own a majority of all the imprints you have on your bookshelf. If you don't trust me, open the copyright page of any book, and many will fess up right there to being owned by one of the Motherships. Motherships are as follows:

- **Penguin/Random House**
- **Hachette Book Group**

- **Harper Collins**
- **Simon and Schuster**
- **Macmillan** (I know—for being one of the Motherships, I hadn't heard much about her either.)

In 2001, Penguin and Random House merged to become a powerhouse publisher, taking the Big Six down to five. In 2020, the publishing world flipped again when it was announced that Penguin/Random House was going to acquire Simon and Schuster, making it the Big Four. As of writing this, the acquisition still hasn't officially happened because people are (rightly so) concerned about the implications of authors getting paid and the growing monopoly of the industry. The more the Motherships merge, the harder it will be to get a book deal, or on an agent's part, to negotiate for a larger advance or royalty.

Have hope: there are still some wonderful independent publishers that are powerhouse publishers. I'm holding out hope that they won't be acquired, and yet, with how tight the financial margins can be in publishing, it's no wonder that when a Mother offers her open arms, many publishers jump at the opportunity to be cradled.

Continuing the uncomfortable image, we come to the arms of Daddy Bezos. That's right, you're Little Author Annie and you need Daddy Bezos to make your book dreams come true. Here's the good news: it's the twenty-first century, and nobody needs a sugar daddy, *buttttt*, Daddy Bezos has set up one of the easiest ways to get published: Amazon KDP for self-publishers. Do it quickly, and you can get your book on a platform where you can utilize the audience they've created to reach readers who you might normally not have access to.

Still, the little penguin, or some other book spine image, may be a dream you've had since you laid in bed as a kid and read until your parents made you turn out the light. If that's the case, dream big! You've already done a ton of work to help you get closer and closer to making this a reality. The following questions in the next section will help you decide if and how to follow through on those publishing steps.

# CHOOSE YOUR OWN ADVENTURE
## QUESTIONS TO ASK TO FIGURE OUT WHAT PUBLISHING PATH IS BEST FOR YOU

Don't overthink this part, and try to answer as honestly as possible!

1.  When you were writing the Comparable Works section, was that difficult or did you feel like there were a lot of books similar to yours?

2.  When you think of your book being published, are you needing it to come out sooner than later? (i.e. If it's something that adds credibility to your work, benefits your company, etc.)

3.  As you imagine the creative elements of your book, how important is it that you control exactly how it looks and feels?

4.  On a scale of one to ten, how important is the stamp of a publisher imprint to you? Be honest.

5.  How much of your book have you shared with others? What has been the feedback?

6.  Is your platform (social media, email list, podcasts, speaking engagements, etc.) actively growing and do you enjoy that aspect of being a writer?

7.  Is this the only book you want to put into the world, or is writing multiple books something you imagine doing?

8.  Have you interacted with any literary agents that have shown interest?

9. Do you have a budget for self-publishing, or is a publishing advance the only way you could get your book into the world?

10. Have you ever said, "I'm just writing this book for me"?

## MY RESPONSE TO YOUR ANSWERS:

### 1. COMPARABLE WORKS

- If it was difficult to find comparable works, that may be a sign that your book is something no one else is writing about. If your story or topic is so compelling and unique that when others hear about it they demand to know more, then you should give traditional publishing a shot.

- There is a difference between being inspired by something and then trying to write your own version of a popular book. It doesn't mean you shouldn't try traditional publishing, but imagine yourself as a publisher after the success of *Eat, Pray, Love*. When the 10,000 proposals claiming to be the next Elizabeth Gilbert come across your desk, inevitably your eyes might start to glaze over. Self-publishing may be a way to let the words speak for themselves, and then you may get noticed by a traditional publisher for your subsequent books.

### 2. TIMELINE

- If traditional publishing is your goal, and you aren't set on publishing this year, then this is a viable option. However, once you sign a contract, you will be more at the mercy of the publisher's timeline than your own. Make sure your agent negotiates the time you need to finish your book. Once you turn it in, there will still be at least a year before it hits the shelves.

- If you are writing a book and need or want it to get published quickly, self-publishing is the way to go. Depending on your commitment to editing, aesthetics, and marketing, you could upload something and have it self-published yesterday. Recently, I ordered a coloring book for my daughter without looking too closely and when it arrived, it was so poorly put together with no complete images that I realized even a drunk person can self-publish. BUT, drunk self-publishing has a short shelf life. If you want to be successful at self-publishing long term, you *will* need to put in time and resources to doing it well and putting out a product that is accurately advertised. The internet review department can make or break your sales, so be honest and do something you would be proud to have your name on, because it will!

## 3. CREATIVE

- If you don't have a creative vision for this book and would rather have someone else make the decisions, traditional publishing will work for you. It doesn't mean you won't have a say in the creative process, but you won't get final say. Unless you're Maya Angelou.

- If creative control is very important to you and you know exactly what you want, you need to clearly lay that out in a proposal and make sure your agent negotiates your involvement, or self-publish. And in this case, if those elements are full color, hardback, etc., then Daddy Bezos (Amazon, if you haven't figured out who I'm referencing) hasn't traditionally gotten the best reviews for full color books. Their paper options are limited and the hardback option is just starting to roll out. This could change, but you may want to check into printers near you where you could touch and feel the quality of their publishing and do a print run that way. Downside is that, unlike print on demand services, distribution will be up to you. It can also be pricey because they will typically have minimum print orders (think 250 copies), so make sure you have a real-life sugar daddy, mommy, or your thirteen-year-old Instagram influencer child who gets 50k per sponsored post to fund your project. (Every night when I put my two-year old daughter to bed, I whisper in her ear as I shut off her ring light, "Sweet dreams baby girl. And don't forget that I expect you to financially support Mommy and Daddy in ten years or less.")

## 4. IMPRINT

- If a well-known imprint is important, then you know what you need to do.

- If it's only the imprint that you want but it doesn't matter who, you can do that yourself! (Details on that under the Self-Publishing Timelines and Goals list.)

## 5. FEEDBACK

- If tons of people who have read your work or heard about your message are clamoring for more, give traditional publishing a shot. Sales and distribution is one of the greatest strengths to traditional publishing, so if you have people wanting your work, publishers can get it to them.

- If you *think* tons of people will clamor for more once they read your book, but you don't quite know for sure, self-publishing can be a way to get the book into the world and start getting feedback. Did you know that with print on demand services, you can go in and make ongoing changes to your book? That is something that can't easily be done with traditional publishing. But again, even though you can make the changes, you still want to put your best foot forward, so invest in cover design, editing, and feedback from writing groups or other respected writers whom you could ask to give your book a read. (And if they aren't close personal friends, I highly recommend offering to pay them for their time and feedback or send a nice gift. If they are a writer or in the publishing industry, they probably get asked this a lot!)

### 6. PLATFORM

- If you are a "content creator" and have a large platform, an agent could probably get a pretty nice advance and royalty battle going for you. My challenge to you is to make sure you don't put something out into the world just because you have a platform. You still probably only have one good "first impression," and if you don't deliver on your first go, it's probably going to fall flat for subsequent deals.

- If you don't have a big platform, don't completely write off getting a traditional book deal. For one, if you write fiction books, there's less concern about platform. For a first-time author, if the story is compelling, an acquiring fiction editor may take a chance.

- If you have a big platform and are getting publishing offers, you still may want to consider self-publishing. It used to have the connotation of being just for authors who couldn't "get real deals," but that is no longer the case. And if the Big Five becomes Big Four and then Big Three, you may see this more and more.

- If you don't have a big platform and have no interest in trying to grow it anyway, self-publishing is going to put the least amount of pressure on you to share about your book release. In the words of literary Sinatra, *you can do it your way.*

### 7. CAREER

- This actually doesn't impact which route you should take. I simply think it's an important question for you to honestly ask yourself so that you can confidently and clearly speak about yourself, the type of author you are, and what this book is to you.

### 8. INTEREST

- If you've had serious interest from a literary agent, and you aren't in a rush, I would give traditional publishing a shot. See if they can get you any offers from traditional publishers and if any of those offers interest you. You are under no obligation to take any of those offers (unless you sign a contract with them that says you are, but I can't imagine that . . .) If you don't like the offers, you can always circle back and do self-publishing (or hybrid publishing, which is often where you pay a company to do everything for you—many are great, but some can be a little scammy, so read reviews.)

- If you've reached out to multiple agents multiple times and heard nothing back, then I would consider either finding publishers that take submissions without an agent (but those will be smaller, potentially unknown imprints who may take the rights to your book) or self-publish and keep the rights to yourself. A self-published book that gets enough traction and popularity could catch the eye of an agent or traditional publisher!

## 9. BUDGET

- A big incentive to get a traditional deal is an advance. Customarily, an advance is given to help support the authors' finances as they write. Just remember though, you will most likely get your advance in two or three payments: at the signing of the contract, manuscript acceptance, and publication of the book. So, that big chunk of an advance will probably get sent to you over the course of twelve to twenty-four months. After that, your royalties don't kick in until your advance is earned back from the sales of your book. Many traditionally published authors don't ever see royalties.

- If you want the *potential* for money NOW, upload your book and start selling. Print on demand can get you royalties immediately. While that sounds enticing, many authors forget to calculate costs of getting the book ready. Sure, you can upload a book with a cover done from Clip Art, but you should consider a budget for editing, design, more editing, marketing, launch strategy, etc. Many people spend between 5k-25k to self-publish a book well. You don't have to pay for all these services, but many people end up hiring contractors, so if you don't budget, it can add up quickly. Just wanted to give you the heads up!

## *10.* GOALS

- If you answered yes to writing for yourself, then I would argue that maybe you don't really need the validation of a publishing imprint or the immediate payout from self-publishing. Maybe you just needed to write the book, work through the process, and have something to hand your kids. If that's the case, don't give Momma Penguin or Daddy Bezos any of the pie. Find an online printing service like IngramSpark or Barnes and Noble Press and order the number of copies you want. Or, as previously mentioned, if you need to touch and feel what it will look like, try to find a local printer. Just don't forget your wheelbarrow full of cash. (I'm being dramatic, they don't all cost an arm and a leg. Just maybe a leg.)

My guess is because you have come this far, most of you want more than just your relatives a few generations from now to read your book. It feels like something you want to put into the world now, and that's great motivation.

This list should help you make a more informed decision based on the different investments you will need to make in both paths. Whichever one you choose, I can promise you it's *all* an adventure! Don't forget that on the frustrating days.

## QUERY LETTERS AND CONTACTING AGENTS

If you have completed these questions and know that traditional publishing is the path for you, some literary agents will first want a query letter before deciding to look through a whole book proposal. Your first step is to research agents you're interested in working with. You can Google your book's genre and "literary agents" to see what results come up, or you can look at comparable books to your own and see who represented them.

Make sure to read the literary agency instructions about how to make contact. They might have an electronic form on their website for prospective authors to fill out, they might want you to submit a query letter, or even just send your full proposal.

In all cases, it's smart to have a query letter on file that's ready to go and send to agencies you're interested in if they ask for one. In your query letter, introduce yourself, your book's concept and vision, and let agents know that you have an already-completed proposal or other specific requests. If you have done everything in this book so far, I'm confident you'll have what they are looking for. Another idea is to record a video-version of your query letter, which can be more interesting and personal than a long and formal query letter (more on that below).

Typically, agents will also have somewhere on their site how long you can expect to wait for a response from them, if at all. Don't feel defeated if you don't hear back, but that's why the more you are prepared with something professional that stands out, the more likely you are to hear back from an agent with next steps.

# CAN WE GET A LITTLE PERSONAL?
## HEADSHOTS, WEBSITE, VIDEOS, AND ART

### HEADSHOTS

It's picture day!!!

*Sounds great, Joy. I've got my scoliosis brace tightened and my retainer locked and loaded.*

Don't panic if you aren't one of those Instagrammers who somehow has a professional photographer on hand at all times to catch the perfectly lit shot of your kids jumping on the bed, or the pensive "pencil in mouth" thinking shot at your desk. If you need a headshot and don't have a ton of extra cash, spend the money on editing your book and use a phone to take your author shot. (Unless you plan for your author shot to be blown up to billboard proportions.) This is how it's done:

- Find anyone who owns a smartphone.

- Make sure they are not my mother.

- Stand facing a window that has good natural light (aka, not at 9:30 p.m.).

- If the phone has a portrait mode, set it to that.

- Try to wear a solid color shirt or something that won't distract from your beautiful face.

- Take a few different shots. (Or 20 or 30 or 400. We aren't working with film, people!) Try one smiling with teeth, one with no teeth, a more straight-faced shot if that's your jam, one where the photographer tells you a joke and then captures you right after you've laughed, and one when you stop to think about the best meal you've ever had. I find those really deliver a nice mix of thoughtful and happy photos, unless, of course, the bill for that meal was far greater than expected.

- Choose the best "that pizza in Italy changed my life" photo and use it on your Amazon Author Page, proposal, back of the book, or wherever!

## WEBSITE

The internet is not going away, and it happens to be one of your greatest business cards. I recently heard about a college that doesn't let students graduate without a personal site. I highly recommend you get something up on the interweb, even if it's a simple landing page that allows people to contact you via email.

Purchase a website domain that is yourname.com, not the title of your book. If you use the title of your book then it limits you to that site for that book. Don't underestimate your future as a multi-book author!

If you want your site to look beautiful with minimal effort, I recommend Squarespace. It's not wildly expensive and it's much more user friendly than other host sites. If you are looking for incredible Squarespace templates to make your job even easier, check out our friends at Go Live HQ. (But before you buy, email me at authors@punchlineagency.com and I might have a discount code for you!)

## PERSONALIZED VIDEO

If you can, use your phone to make a video introduction to an agent or publisher. Like I mentioned before, this can often be submitted in lieu of a formal query letter. Use their name if you can, and take one to three minutes to introduce yourself and verbalize your Author Vision. If you think you're awkward on camera, it's only because you haven't done it enough.

### [Pro-ish Tips]

- Set your phone in landscape position on a windowsill. (Again, during the day, not night.)

- Put a sticky note with three to five bullet points over the screen so if it's facing you, you don't get distracted while looking at yourself.

- Look at the camera LENS, not the screen itself.

- Right before you hit record, stand up, spread your feet as wide as you can, put your arms in the air so you look like a big human X and take a few deep breaths. Then, fake or real laugh and hit record. Trust me, when you start talking, you'll have a much more natural disposition.

- If you don't know how to edit off the few seconds at the beginning where you're trailing off from fake laughing or the end of a video where your arm is reaching across the screen to hit the record button, have your nearest teenager do it for you.

## ART

Some of the authors I have worked with are artists or have worked with artists to add a design element to make their proposal stand out. If you do opt for creating a more design-heavy proposal, note the following as you make your decision:

- Does this design help clarify or confuse what I'm trying to communicate?

- Is it clear if these are simply design elements for the proposal, or am I communicating that they are part of my book?

- If I invest the time and resources into adding art or design work to my proposal, I understand that I may not be able to submit it in that form to some agents or publishers because of their uploading requirements. WaaaaaWahhhhhhh.

# NOW, THIS

## TIMELINES FOR HITTING YOUR GOALS

If you've bought this book, then you're ready to knock things out—quickly. If you've completed all of this work in 30 days, you can reach your dominant hand high into the sky and then cross over the shoulder of your less dominant hand and give yourself a big ole pat on the back.

BRAVO, MY FRIEND.

*If I'm being honest, it actually took me 47 days, Joy.*

Pat away anyway. Do you know how many people talk about writing a book and never sit down to actually do the work? Not to mention all the extra necessary things that go with writing a book, like summaries, marketing, and designing the $29.99 cookie jar that Williams Sonoma will sell to go along with your book?

*I don't get that reference.*

THEN I DON'T GET HOW YOU CAN CLAIM YOU ACTUALLY READ THIS BOOK!

*Oh yeah, the Frozen empire reference. I remember now. C'mon, that was a deep cut. I can't remember every word of brilliance you've crafted.*

Go on . . .

*No, you go on. I want to know what timelines I should set for myself.*

OK, so it depends on which publishing adventure you've decided to take and truly how motivated you are, but here are some estimated timelines based on my professional experience and guessing-pertise:

## TRADITIONAL PUBLISHING ESTIMATED TIMELINES

### PROPOSAL AND SAMPLE CHAPTERS EDITS

You've already got all the content from going through this book! Editing and typesetting your proposal is optional, but it will only help clarify your text and check for errors.

*TIMELINES:*

Developmental "Dev" Edits: 1-6 weeks
Copy Edits: 1-2 weeks
Proofreading: 1-2 weeks
Typeset: 1-2 weeks

### AGENT SUBMISSIONS

Research to find agents you like, submit their required materials, wait for their response, and then, hopefully, sign with an agent! After you sign, you will work together on recommended proposal changes and preparatory work before pitching to publishers.

*TIMELINE:*

1 week–?

### PUBLISHERS

Your agent will pitch with a due date for publishers to make offers by. When an offer comes in, your agent should present the different options and pros and cons of each publisher, while negotiating on your behalf to strengthen the offer. When you settle on an offer, you sign with the publisher, and work with them during the next twelve to twenty-four months until your publishing date. This timeline is often determined by:

- Percentage of book completed at signing (yes, you do have to finish writing the actual book—make sure you factor that in . . .).

- What time of year your book's release would be most strategic with your audience.

- What other titles the publisher is releasing and avoiding conflicting marketing.

## TIMELINES:
Pitching: 5-6 weeks
Offers: 1-4 weeks
Author signs: 1-3 seconds, depending on how fast you write your name
Book releases: 12-24 months after contract is signed

## BOOK RELEASE

Hit all the best seller lists and travel the world unable to dine in peace without strangers interrupting the first bite of your Dragon Roll to tell you that your book changed their life. You set your chopsticks down, pick up your Saki glass and give a humble nod of gratitude. Unfortunately, they misinterpret your kind smile as an invitation to pull up a chair and bring over their Saki glass.

## TIMELINE:
Forever years after book release.

# TRADITIONAL PUBLISHING CHECKLIST AND GOALS

Fill in the table with specific tasks as you plan out your publishing goals, checking them off as you accomplish them!

| ✓ | TASK | GOAL DATE |
|---|------|-----------|
| | | |
| | | |
| | | |
| | | |
| | | |
| | | |
| | | |
| | | |
| | | |
| | | |
| | | |
| | | |
| | | |
| | | |
| | | |
| | | |
| | | |
| | | |

# SELF-PUBLISHING ESTIMATED TIMELINES

## FINISH THE BOOK

Your first step is to write your book! How long it takes authors to write changes from person to person; sometimes it takes months, oftentimes it takes years. I believe you can do it in six months. Here's why:

Since you've already written at least three sample chapters, think about how long those took you to actually write. When you sat down, how many hours did you put in? Consider this way of viewing your writing time as opposed to saying, "I wrote these over the course of three months." Then, look at your calendar and, based off of your writing style (daily habit vs. writing retreat), block off times on your calendar over the next six months and have someone hold you accountable! Do the work. You've come so far; you can do it.

*TIMELINE:*

Up to the author

*MONTHS BEFORE PUBLICATION:*

3-12 months

## DEVELOPMENTAL AND COPY EDITING

Just as we recommend hiring editors to look over your proposal, you should definitely hire an editor (or two) to look at your whole book to ensure there is clarity and organization throughout your book.

*TIMELINE:*

2-8 weeks, depending on manuscript length

*MONTHS BEFORE PUBLICATION:*

3-4 months

## FINAL PROOFREADING

This is most beneficial when it's a new editor with a new set of eyes to see the things that can be difficult for the author and even other editors to catch after they've been in the manuscript so many times.

*TIMELINE:*

1-4 weeks

*MONTHS BEFORE PUBLICATION:*

3-4 months

## TITLING AND SEO

Remember to devote some time to evaluate your book's SEO, so it's easy for your audience (and potential audience) to find it! During this stage, you can hire someone or use a program like Publisher Rocket to evaluate key phrases, categories, titles, and descriptions before you decide what to name and how to describe your book online.

*TIMELINE:*

1-2 weeks

*MONTHS BEFORE PUBLICATION:*

2-3 months

## ENDORSEMENTS

Send out a few sample chapters to the people you want to endorse your book, and, depending on how tight your timeline is, if you have a mockup of the cover design, send that to them as well. I recommend sending a personal email and including the following:

- Use either your one sentence summary or half-page summary to tell them about your book.

- Tell them the date you want an endorsement by and the launch date or tentative release date.

- Ask them for one to three lines of endorsement and the way they want their name listed and either a book title of something they've written or their work title.

*TIMELINE:*

1-2 weeks

*MONTHS BEFORE PUBLICATION:*

2-3 months

## ARCS

ARC stands for Advanced Reader Copy. Traditional publishers will send these out on your behalf, but if you are self-publishing or publishing through a print on demand service (what Amazon does, which means they print a copy of your book when it's purchased), then you will want to consider ordering a bulk number of copies of your book in advance of your launch date. You can do this through print on demand services but they will usually limit you to ordering about five copies at a time and there is a big line that says "NOT FOR RESALE" on the cover. I recommend getting 50-250 copies printed when the book is 100 percent ready to go by an independent printer. Then, you can mail those copies out to people who endorsed your book, or a book launch team, in advance of the book coming out. This way, on the launch day, they already have them in hand and you can make a follow-up request that they share a photo or review on that day.

*TIMELINE:*

2-4 weeks (depending on print time)

*MONTHS BEFORE PUBLICATION:*

1-3 months

# BOOK LAUNCH TEAM

There are many ways to gather a book launch team, but I think the best way is to find a mix of personal friends and family as well as influencers and other writers. You can invite people personally, on social media, or in additional platforms you might have, like a newsletter, podcast, etc. You can put a cap on the number of people you'll have on your launch team if you want to make it feel exciting and exclusive. Anywhere from fifteen to seventy-five people who have either endorsed your book or are fans of you will help to share and tell their people about your book. You don't want to overwhelm them, but you should be organized in giving them information that will make sharing easier for them. Here are some things you can do:

- Send them an ARC and include a personal note and even a gift of gratitude for reading the book in advance.

- Include instructions of what you'd like them to share and when.

- Follow up on or around the launch day with ideas for what they can share online and how much it would mean to you.

- Give them links for where to leave reviews.

*TIMELINE:*
................
4 weeks

*MONTHS BEFORE PUBLICATION:*
.................................................
1-2 months

# BOOK DESIGN AND TYPESETTING

One of the "this is actually happening" moments is when you get to see the design, colors, and images for your book coming to life. As your book edits start to wrap up, it will be time to look into finding someone to create your dream book design. While exterior designers will work on your cover, spine, and back design, an interior designer may work on formatting, illustrations, size, layout, and typesetting.

3-6 weeks

1-4 months (depending on how much pre-hype you want to build by giving people sneak peeks of your cover)

## LEGAL SETUP AND PUBLISHING IMPRINT

One of the final steps before you can release your book in the world is to complete the legal aspects of publishing a book. Womp-womp.

## ISBN

In America, the only place to purchase an ISBN (the code above the barcode on the back of your book) is from Bowker's at myidentifiers.com. In a free market society, I'm not sure why Billy Bob Bowker got the monopoly on ISBNs, but he did. You can also buy barcodes from them. It's not mandatory to have a barcode on your book, but it allows your book to be read by a machine, which increases your chances of getting your book sold at brick-and-mortar stores that require a barcode. Companies like Amazon's KDP will often add a barcode if you do not.

## COPYRIGHT

If you want to buy a copyright with the U.S. Copyright Office (which many authors do not), you can register at copyright.gov. Purchasing your copyright registers the work with the U.S. Copyright Office and allows you to file a copyright infringement lawsuit if your work is ever infringed upon. However, as a self-published author, your writing is copyrighted simply by putting pen to paper. You can find many templates online (I love Reedsy. com), but if all you do is write the following, it makes your copyright official and is absolutely free to do:

Copyright © [INSERT YEAR] [YOUR NAME]
All rights reserved.

## PUBLISHING IMPRINT

This isn't mandatory, and many self-published authors simply list their last name or no publisher at all, but if you decide to start your own imprint, you need to decide on an imprint name and create an LLC. Then, you need to make sure the same name hasn't been established in your state already. You could hire a designer to create an imprint logo, or, if you have it in you, create something in a user-friendly platform such as Canva.

*TIMELINE:*

2 weeks

*MONTHS BEFORE PUBLICATION:*

2 weeks-3 months

## AMAZON AUTHOR PAGE

With an Amazon Author Central Page, readers will be able to find information about your and other publications in one spot. If you already have a book on Amazon, you can start an author page now. However, if you are a first-time author, you'll have to wait until you submit your book to Amazon to create your page.

> *[Note] Make sure your name is written exactly as you want it for your book and Amazon Author Central page. If you have a typo, change of name, or middle name in your author name, it should be the exact same for your Amazon Central Page if you want people to find your book.*

2 weeks

2 weeks-3 months

## LAUNCH STRATEGY, MARKETING PLAN, AND PR

As you prepare to put your book into the world, you will want to start bringing in people who will help you prepare a marketing and launch strategy. Each book release should have a pre-launch, launch, and post-launch plan. If you aren't a marketing or PR mastermind yourself, many authors reach out to professionals to help out with this step.

*TIMELINE:*

Ongoing

*MONTHS BEFORE PUBLICATION:*

1-6 months before and after publishing date

Before you start breathing into a paper bag, remember, you don't have to plan a launch strategy or do all the things, but if you want to get the word out about your book, it's pretty vital—for both traditional and self-published authors.

# SELF- PUBLISHING CHECKLIST AND GOALS

Fill in the table with specific tasks as you plan out your publishing goals, checking them off as you accomplish them!

| ✓ | TASK | GOAL DATE |
|---|------|-----------|
| | | |
| | | |
| | | |
| | | |
| | | |
| | | |
| | | |
| | | |
| | | |
| | | |
| | | |
| | | |
| | | |
| | | |
| | | |
| | | |
| | | |
| | | |

# AU REVOIR!

## CALL ME, ANYTIME

Well, friend (and I do hope you feel like we are friends at this point),

*I do.*

You have come a *long* way. I truly hope and pray that you feel more confident in the ever-changing world of publishing. However, something that doesn't change is that if you do write, and keep writing, you are in fact a writer. Somehow, because we know of the "greats," it's easy to let Doubting Darla in and whisper, "You can't do this."

Remember in the beginning when I quoted the beloved statement about writers, "Writers love to have written"? Writing is hard, for sure, but I also think it's possible, because you bought this book, that there is a part of you that loves to write. Maybe even has *FUN* writing. Let's get this angsty writer image out of our head and do what is one of my favorite pastimes . . .

# HAVE FUN.

Call me, anytime.[6]

Love,

Joy

---

6    International rates do apply. So maybe just email . . . authors@punchlineagency.com

# WHEN YOU BUY THIS BOOK

For every copy of this book sold, a child waiting in a DHS (Department of Human Services) office awaiting placement in the foster care system will receive their very own copy of *Writing with Bernard The Baguette: A Kids (Fun and Silly) Guide to Discover the Joys of Writing*.

We created this guide specifically for elementary-aged kids who enjoy writing and want to learn more, or kids who are scared to write because it feels daunting and un-fun. *Bernard The Baguette* leads kids through prompts and fun activities to get their writing wheels turning. They will learn about creative writing, memoir, and journalism.

Our hope for the children in DHS offices is that the guide will help them find some sense of ownership and stability through the craft of writing during a time when they are feeling extreme levels of uncertainty.

Additionally, you can pick up a copy of Bernard for the little in your life, or if you are a teacher and would like to place an order for your whole class, email authors@punchlineagency.com to learn more about discounts and bulk ordering.

We have partnered with Every Child Oregon, who will distribute the guides to DHS offices all throughout the state of Oregon.

everychildoregon.org

If you have an organization in your state that would be able to partner with their DHS offices for distribution, please let us know.

# ABOUT PUNCHLINE AGENCY

Punchline is an agency founded by Joy Eggerichs Reed to support people who are good on the page and the stage. Everything we do is to amplify the voices and messages that we believe need to be heard. We do this in three distinct ways:

## SPEAKING

We started as a speaking agency and still hold tight to our values of representing voices with something important to say. Some names you might know, some you might not——but we believe in ALL of them, and know the importance of bringing the right person to various events.

## LITERARY

We take on a certain number of books each year and guide authors through the process of a book proposal and pitching to traditional publishers. We've also started Punchline Publishers, which supports authors who are seeking an alternative to traditional publishing.

## CONSULTING

Want more accountability and human interaction? We have live courses, small group cohorts and individual consultations. We can give feedback on book ideas, review proposals, fine-tune keynotes, punch up the humor for your next presentation and be your emotional support. And like this book, we give tangible (and slightly aggressive) action plans to accomplish your goals.

*Visit punchlineagency.com to learn more.*

# ABOUT THE ILLUSTRATOR

Kristin McNess Moran has always been a maker and artist, naturally and intuitively communicating through illustration and type, mainly in water-color and mixed media. Whether fashioning animal artwork out of duct tape for those closest to her or reimagining vintage ball gowns into floor-length costumery, she is able to naturally renew and reinvent her art for whatever the occasion. She's a great friend to have at Halloween.

Having studied fashion design and illustration at Washington University in St. Louis, her career took her all the way to senior apparel designer at Adidas where she worked on everything from kidswear to NBA apparel for both universal wear (you and me) all the way to the elite players like Damian Lillard. (Go Blazers!)

Kristin is a voracious reader especially of Young Adult fantasy fiction, her favorites being: Sarah J. Maas's Throne of Glass series, The Name of the Wind by Patrick Rothfuss, and of course, Harry Potter.

She resides in Portland, Oregon in a modern commune with great friends, an aspiring gardener husband, and two little girls.

# ABOUT THE AUTHOR

Joy Eggerichs Reed is the founder of Punchline Agency: A literary and speaking agency for people good on the page and stage. Aside from managing and negotiating on behalf of authors and speakers, Joy consults with aspiring writers, speakers, and those seeking to clarify a message or idea.

Prior to being an agent, Joy got her start as a blogger and speaker, creating over 500 written and video posts and speaking to audiences of up to 12k people on the topic of singleness and relationships. In 2014, Christianity Today named Joy one of 33 leaders under the age of 33 shaping the next generation. In 2017, Joy launched Punchline Agency to represent and develop communicators and voices she believed needed to be heard.

She currently resides as an expat in Paris, France with her husband Matt and two petite bébés, Millie and Emerson. Collectively, their family consumes thirty-four percent of the country's croissant production.

# SPECIAL THANKS

To "The Putonians," also known as my first cohort of five who went through this content and made me realize how fun it is to become friends with strangers from the internet. Look what Mother Hen did!

To Holly, thank you for believing whole heartedly in Punchline and for being the best kind of scrappy. As John D. Rockefeller said, "a friendship founded on business is a good deal better than a business founded on friendship." Thank you for becoming one of my dearest friends.

To Kristin, thank you for first designing my over-the-top flower crown dreams for my wedding and now designing the perfect illustrations for "our" book. This book is 100X better with your old lady giving a wink or two.

To Amelia, thank you for your upbeat attitude, edits, feedback, and **all** the research for getting this book legal and ready for the world. If you don't get KDP tattooed somewhere, I will consider that a fail.

To Sarah Cybulski, thank you for coming in the final hour for a thorough proofread! I'm sorry I have such a horrific understanding and usage, of, the, comma.

To Stephanie Smith and Elizabeth Passarella, thank you for being two people I wildly admire in this industry and taking the time amidst your own editing and writing to give me thoughtful and helpful feedback. [Insert me bowing in the same way I would to Her Majesty.]

To Paige Smith, thank you for being the queen of self-publishing and being such an encouraging light and resource to me and the whole Punchline team. If you ever decide to dabble into non-fiction, let me know. I have an idea. [wink]

To my parents who welcomed all four of us back to Michigan "for a few weeks in November while the pandemic settles down in Paris." (I'm writing this on April 8, 2021, still in Michigan.) Your life-long belief in me plus almost six months of FREE DAYCARE made this book possible. (Guess you guys are a little more socialist than you thought, huh!?)

To Scott and Jen, my parents' next door neighbors who let us make their house our home for a while. As I write this I am sitting at the folding table I bought at Meijer and set in front of your bedroom window. Ironically, I've written both of my books (this one and the one I mentioned in the beginning of this book) in your home. If this becomes a pattern, you guys might need to claim a percentage of my book earnings. (I know an agent.)

To Frugthaven Farm, the coffee shop that kept me caffeinated and cozy. April Peterson, I don't know what you give your baristas, but everyone is always happy and friendly and when I let my black coffee get cold, they just give me a fresh new cup. (Wait, maybe they aren't supposed to do that . . .)

To Millie and Emerson, if I never write another book, I want to make sure your names get in here. Thanks for always greeting me with a smile and flailing arms when I "stopped in to say Bonjour" at Mimi's Creche. That was actually just Emerson. Millie, you were a little more fifty-fifty on enthusiasm upon seeing my face, but I'll take what I can get.

To my husband Matt, I would write something really mushy but I don't want to make everyone uncomfortable. You're my favorite human and your belief in me is wildly disproportionate, but I'll take it all. Thank you for picking up the slack when this extra plate started spinning faster than I had anticipated. Also, I look forward to reading (and agenting) the book you write one day.

# BIBLIOGRAPHY

**Page 26:**

Hemingway, Ernest. *A Moveable Feast*. Reprint ed. New York: Scribner, 2010.

**Page 28:**

Plimpton, George. "Ernest Hemingway, The Art of Fiction No. 21." *The Paris Review*, issue 18, Spring 1958. Accessed April 14, 2021. https://www.theparisreview.org/interviews/4825/the-art-of-fiction-no-21-ernest-hemingway.

Knox, Elizabeth. "Sustainable Pace at Work." Unpublished manuscript, last modified April 16, 2021. Microsoft Word file

**Page 35:**

Westfall, Chris. "Origins of the Elevator Pitch." Chris Westfall. May 30, 2013. Accessed April 14, 2021, https://bit.ly/3djA3Za.

**Page 36:**

Keith, Sue. "An Elevator Pitch—Inside an Elevator." Ceres Talent. February 15, 2016. Accessed April 14, 2021. https://cerestalent.com/an-elevator-pitch-inside-an-elevator/.

**Page 41:**

Lewis, C.S. *The Lion, The Witch, and The Wardrobe*. The Chronicles of Narnia. New York: HarperCollins, 2008.

**Page 42:**

Boden, Leah. *Modern Miss Mason: Sharing Charlotte Mason with a New Generation*. Carol Stream: Tyndale House Publishers, forthcoming.

**Page 45:**

Alcott, Louisa May. *Little Women*. Boston: Roberts Brothers, 1868.

**Page 53:**

Alcott, *Little Women*.

**Page 60:**

Gladwell, Malcolm. *Talking to Strangers: What We Should Know About the People We Don't Know*. New York: Little, Brown, and Company, 2019.

**Page 62:**

Faber, Adele and Elaine Mazlish. *How to Talk So Kids will Listen, and Listen So Kids will Talk*. New York: Scribner, 2012.

**Page 76:**

Cirillo, Francesco. "The Pomodoro Technique." Francesco Cirillo. Cirillo Consulting. 2021, Accessed April 14, 2021. https://francescocirillo.com/pages/pomodoro-technique/

**Page 95:**

Bohannon, Liz Forkin. "#28 Matthew McConaughey on Guilt, Shame, and How Responsibility Breeds True Freedom." Produced by Hueman Group Media. *Plucking Up with Liz Forkin Bohannon*, March 15, 2021. Podcast. http://lizbohannon.co/plucking-up/.

**Page 118:**

Collins, Suzanne. *The Hunger Games*. Hunger Games Trilogy. New York: Scholastic Press, 2009.

**Page 119:**

Condie. Ally. *Matched*. Matched Trilogy. New York: Penguin Books, 2011.

Roth, Veronica. *Divergent*. Divergent Trilogy. New York: Katherine Tegen Books, 2011.

**Page 120:**

Dashner, James. *The Maze Runner*. The Maze Runner Series. New York: Delacorte Press, 2009.

**Page 121:**

Fitzgerald, F. Scott. The Great Gatsby. New York: Charles Scribner's Sons, 1925.

Covey, Stephen R. *The 7 Habits of Highly Effective People*. 4th ed. New York: Simon & Schuster, 2020.

**Page 128:**

Zusak, Markus. *The Book Thief*. New York: Knopf Books for Young Readers, 2007.

Niffenegger, Audrey. *The Time Traveler's Wife*. San Francisco: MacAdam/Cage, 2003.

**Page 135:**

Rowling, J.K. *Harry Potter and the Sorcerer's Stone*. New York: Scholastic, 1998.

Collins, Jim. Good to Great: *Why Some Companies Make the Leap and Others Don't*. New York: HarperBusiness, 2001.

Made in the USA
Columbia, SC
02 October 2022

68526359R00109